"I recommend this book as I believe it takes seriously the vital warnings which God gives us all at the close of the Book of Revelation, in chapter 22 verses 18 and 19. Here, we are told by God that we must not add to the Bible nor must we subtract from it. If we do either the one or the other God will punish us severely. The Bible, the whole Bible and nothing but the Bible is God's inspired revelation to mankind. This we should believe and by this rule should we live. It is in this way that we shall honour and glorify God. Only in this way shall we be living as God requires us all to live."

Maurice Roberts, Retired Editor, *The Banner of Truth Magazine*

"The single-most important doctrinal issue facing Christianity today is restoring the Doctrine of God's Providential Preservation of His Word. Because of modern Textual Criticism, this age-old doctrine has been pushed aside and is no longer present in most of the Church Confessions today. As a result, the world is flooded with numerous new translations of the Bible that have caused confusion and doctrinal error. Has God providentially preserved His Holy Word? The answer in this book is a resounding 'Yes!' and is convincingly explained and defended in many essays by pastor-scholars who hold to the Traditional Text of Scripture. This book is the clarion call for the church to return to the text that has sustained Christianity and preserved truth for centuries - the Traditional, or Ecclesiastical text. This book is also a warning that by using an impoverished translation of Scripture, weak preaching and bad theology will result. It is a must-read for every pastor committed to truth."

Dr. James E. Bearss, Professor, Seminario Reformado Latinoamericano, President, On Target Ministry

"The 'house of the Lord' (Psalm 27:4) has always been the best place to do theology. More valuable than a seminary's clinical evaluation of Scriptural texts, this anthology contains multiple compelling cases for the superiority of the Received Text set in a doxological context. With confessional pre-commitments firmly in place, within these pages the reader will appreciate how historic, orthodox Protestant theology and apologetics is properly formulated. This volume reinforces the argument for the superiority of the Received Text and challenges the interlocular to reconsider the pusillanimous expressions of the historical critical method. Written to both edify and inform, I heartily recommend it."

Dr. Peter Van Kleeck, Sr., Pastor, Providence Baptist Church (Manassas, Virginia), Former Director, Institute for Biblical and Textual Studies (Grand Rapids, Michigan)

Why I Preach from the Received Text

WHY I PREACH
FROM THE
RECEIVED TEXT

An Anthology of Essays
by Reformed Ministers

Edited by **Jeffrey T. Riddle &**
Christian M. McShaffrey

THE
Greater Heritage
Christian Publishing
Winter Springs, FL

Why I Preach from the Received Text: An Anthology of Essays by Reformed Ministers edited by Jeffrey T. Riddle & Christian M. McShaffrey
These hardcover, paperback and eBook editions first published July 2022
© 2022 The Greater Heritage

Published by The Greater Heritage
            1170 Tree Swallow Dr., Suite 309
            Winter Springs, FL 32708

All scripture references are taken from the King James Version (KJV) of the Bible.

Email: info@thegreaterheritage.com
Website: www.thegreaterheritage.com

Cover Design: The Greater Heritage
Cover Image: *Westminster Abbey and Bridge* (1794) by Joseph Farington, 1747–1821, British. Oil on canvas. Yale Center for British Art. Paul Mellon Collection. B1976.7.28.
Font(s): Adobe Caslon Pro, Alegreya, Calluna, Cardo, Constantia, Vollkorn.

Library of Congress Control Number: 2022910080

ISBN (hardcover): 978-1-953855-79-4
ISBN (paperback): 978-1-953855-90-9
ISBN (PDF): 978-1-953855-88-6
ISBN (EPUB): 978-1-953855-94-7

1 2 3 4 5 6 7 8 9 10   26 25 24 23 22

Contents

Abbreviations

AV	Authorized (King James) Version
CT	Modern Critical Text
ESV	English Standard Version
KJV	King James Version
LBCF	London Baptist Confession of Faith (1689)*
LXX	The Greek Septuagint
NA28	Novum Testamentum Graece, 28th edition
NASB	New American Standard Bible
NRSV	New Revised Standard Version
TNIV	Today's New International Version
TR	*Textus Receptus* (Received Text)
WCF	Westminster Confession of Faith
WSC	Westminster Shorter Catechism

*In this work's citations from LBCF 1.8 the original word "authentical" has been retained, rather than "authentic," which appears in several contemporary printed editions of the LBCF.

Editorial Introduction

Jeffrey T. Riddle & Christian M. McShaffrey

From the beginning, the devil has sought to destroy the souls of men by enticing them to doubt God's Word. Our first father Adam received God's Word through direct revelation in the Garden of Eden. The Lord commanded, "Of every tree of the garden thou mayest freely eat: but of the tree of the knowledge of good and evil, thou shalt not eat of it: for in the day that thou eatest thereof thou shalt surely die" (Genesis 2:16-17). Sadly, on the very next page of Scripture, we witness the devil's first attempt to deceive mankind, when he asked, "Yea, hath God said...?" (Genesis 3:1).

It is a dangerous thing to challenge the integrity and authority of God's Word. It appears that our first mother succumbed to this danger. She tried to answer the enemy of her soul, but made no less than three mistakes in the attempt: Eve modified, added to, and deleted from God's Word.

Eve's modification of Scripture consisted in replacing a singular pronoun with a plural pronoun. She answered the serpent, saying, "Ye shall not eat of it..." (Genesis 3:3) when God had actually said "thou shalt not eat of it" (Genesis 2:17). This was not a major modification. Some might even argue that it was good for her to apply God's direct Word to Adam to herself, but her words, in fact, altered what God had said. She should have responded, as our Savior did when he was tempted in the wilderness, with a direct quotation (cf. Matthew 4:4, 7, 10). Eve proceeded to add to Scripture when she spoke of the forbidden fruit, saying, "neither shall ye touch it..." (Genesis 3:3). God had said no such thing. Perhaps she said it innocently enough (i.e., simply emphasizing how off-limits the fruit was), but this was an addition to what God had said. She should not have responded with her own speculation and emendation. Finally, Eve deleted part of Scripture, saying, "lest ye die" (Genesis 3:3). God had, in fact, said more than that. He spoke with more dreadful severity, saying, "thou shalt surely die" (Genesis 2:17). Eve's omission served to soften the intensity of the divine threat.

Why focus on this single event that occurred thousands of years ago? It proves two things. First, it exposes Satan's subtle strategy for the destruction of souls. He seeks to destroy our faith by casting doubt over God's Word. Second, it demonstrates how susceptible we are to Satan's wiles.

God has raised up men in every generation since the fall and given them the courage needed to rebuke the devil and his servants. There was, in fact, none braver than the Lord Jesus Christ himself, who rebuked the devil with the words, "Get thee behind me, Satan!" (Luke 4:8). Strangely enough, even that saying, found in the Received Text, no longer appears in many modern translations of this verse in the Gospel of Luke, such as the NIV and ESV. This is only one of many examples of places where the modern critics have assumed textual corruption, and then arrogated to themselves the role of being "correctors" of holy writ. Even those who might initially profess to believe the scriptures were originally inspired by God, too often then proceed to deny that God has also preserved that same inspired Word in its transmission.

Modern academic textual criticism rejects divine preservation, and therefore proceeds to pursue reconstruction of the text based on human reasoning. This view of the text of Scripture stands in stark contrast to the Bibliology of the men of the Reformation and post-Reformation (Protestant orthodox) eras. Those godly men maintained that the Lord had not only immediately inspired the Scriptures in the original Hebrew and Greek, but that he had also kept them pure in all ages (cf. WCF and LBCF, 1.8, the most cited confessional passage in this anthology!). This led them to affirm the classic Protestant printed editions of the Masoretic Text of the Hebrew Old Testament and the *Textus Receptus* of the Greek New Testament as the standard text of the Christian Bible. This traditional or Received Text of Scripture provided a faithful touchstone for Protestant, Bible-believing scholars, ministers, churchmen, and congregations as they conducted their ministries. This text was the basis for scholarly study, preaching, and translation of the Bible amongst the Protestant churches.

In the nineteenth century an especially concerted effort was made to undermine the authority of the traditional text and to replace it with the modern critical text. This effort extended into the twentieth century and included the replacement of classic Protestant translations of the Bible in various languages with new translations based on the modern critical text. Admittedly, this movement has been quite successful even among many conservative, evangelical, and Reformed men.

Not all, however, have jumped on the modern critical text band-wagon. Some have raised questions about the faithfulness and the wisdom of abandoning the Protestant touchstone of the traditional biblical text in favor of an ever-shifting modern critical text. They have maintained that we should hold fast to the old text and to the classic Protestant translations based upon it. This anthology provides a sampling of the reasoning which has led such men to this conviction.

We are thankful to the twenty-five men who contributed essays to this work. In seeking contributors to this project, we invited men who were actively serving as officers in local churches. We wanted men who were gladly laboring in the trenches of local church ministry. The authors include Pastors, Teachers, Elders, and one Deacon, coming from Reformed, Presbyterian, and Baptist traditions. These men hail from places across the English-speaking world, including Australia, Canada, the United Kingdom, and the United States. Some of the writers have served for decades in pastoral ministry, while others are young men just beginning their service.

We gave each contributor the same topic to consider, "Why I Preach from the Received Text." In reading these essays it will become clear that all the contributors have high respect for the Authorized or King James Version of the Bible in English, as many make mention of this venerable translation in their respective essays. The reader should not, however, be confused about this book's primary focus. Critics of the traditional text, in fact, often confuse our position, whether intentionally or unintentionally, with "King James Version-Onlyism," a position which is inconsistent with WCF and LBCF 1.8. We did not ask our authors to address, "Why I Preach from the King James Version," but "Why I Preach from the Received Text." The primary purpose of this book is a defense of the traditional original Hebrew and Greek text of the Bible.

As editors, we are pleased with the diversity and strength of these contributions. Some of the essays are personal and autobiographical, while others are more historical and doctrinal, but all reflect the conviction contained in our Protestant Reformed Confessions: God has kept his Word pure in all ages. These essays, offered in alphabetical order by the names of the authors, are written in a popular and easily accessible style. Rather than footnotes, simple and abbreviated references to any works cited appear within the text itself. We hope this will aid the reader who wants to seek out any such references. Since most of the authors are regularly engaged in preaching, many of the essays are written in a homiletical style. Spelling and punctuation have been conformed to the general standards of American English. At the end of the book there is an Appendix titled "Steps Toward Change in Your Church" offering pastoral advice on addressing text in a local congregation. Finally, there is a select annotated bibliography providing resources for the further study of the traditional text.

It is our hope that each reader's confidence in the integrity of Scripture will be increased as he moves through the pages of this book. We particularly desire that those ministers and their congregations who have stood fast in their use of the traditional text, even when it seemed they had few allies and many adversaries, will be encouraged by this work, knowing that they do not stand alone and that this position is neither unreasonable nor obscurantist. It is also our hope that a new generation of young believers and young men called to ministry might be prompted by this work to give careful consideration regarding the text of the Bible they choose to embrace.

We close this introduction with an anecdote from the Puritan author Henry Scougal (1650-1678). In his collected works one finds a series of personal reflections drawn from his private diary (cf. *The Works of Henry Scougal*, 256-257). First, there is a note recorded on November 1, 1668 titled, "On the Sad Report of the Death of a Pious and Learned Friend." As the title indicates, Scougal's note expressed his grief on receiving the news that a dear friend had expired. Scougal movingly wrote: "The purest crystal is soon cracked, while courser metal can endure a stroke. The brittle cage was much too narrow and long to enclose a bird whose soaring wing required a larger volary."

The next note, however, was recorded over a week later and had this title, "On the Sight of the Foresaid Person Whom I Had Concluded to be Dead, November 10, When I Had Occasion to Visit Him at His House." Scougal began this note, "Oh, happy disappointment, to see him yet alive, whom some days ago I had buried in my apprehensions!"

This anecdote calls to mind the quip attributed to Mark Twain, "Reports of my death have been greatly exaggerated." This collection of essays similarly declares that reports of the death of the traditional text of Holy Scripture in the use of faithful churches and among their ministers has been greatly exaggerated. Though it may appear to some that the traditional text has suffered the fate of the traveler on the road to Jericho who "fell among thieves" and was left "half dead" (Luke 10:30), it is, in fact, very much alive. As Gamaliel said of the ministry of the Apostles, "But if it be of God, ye cannot overthrow it; lest haply ye be found even to fight against God" (Acts 5:39). May the Lord use this book as an instrument to stimulate, revive, confirm, and defend intelligent and effective usage of the traditional text of the Word of God.

Jeffrey T. Riddle

Christian M. McShaffrey

1

Infallible Truth, Not Probability

Archibald Allison

The Lord blessed me with growing up in a Christian home and in confessional Reformed churches. God's Word was read and preached regularly more than once a day, and I memorized many passages of Scripture using the King James Version. I read the King James Version of the Bible from the time I learned to read. For almost three decades, I have served as Pastor of a confessional Reformed church in the western United States where there are few Reformed churches, and many know nothing about the Reformed faith.

My father bought a facsimile of the Geneva Bible (1560), which was the first translation of the Bible widely used in the English-speaking world and the primary predecessor of the King James Version (1611). During family worship every day, one member of the family read aloud from the Geneva Bible while my father followed using his Hebrew or Greek Bible, and the rest of the family followed using the King James Version.

My father talked about what was wrong with Westcott and Hort's views of the Greek manuscripts and what he was taught in seminary about textual criticism. A woman in our church enjoyed discussing with my father the important theological and practical aspects of maintaining, defending, and using the Received Text (the Masoretic Text of the Hebrew Old Testament and the *Textus Receptus* of the Greek New Testament).

The King James Version of the Bible was used almost everywhere in the English-speaking world when I was young, including most churches. The Gideons distributed the King James Version of the Bible. There were only a few other English versions of the Bible that were readily available. The liberal churches used the Revised Standard Version of the Bible, published in 1952 by the Division of Christian Education of the National Council of the Churches of Christ in the USA as a revision of the American Standard Version of 1901. The Revised Standard Version is based on a critical text that follows the ideas of Westcott and Hort and those who follow their view of textual criticism.

The Revised Standard Version promoted Modernism, or theological liberalism, which is a form of unbelief, in its translation of God's Word. For example, Isaiah 7:14 in the Revised Standard Version is translated, "Therefore the Lord himself will give you a sign. Behold, a young woman shall conceive and bear a son, and shall call his name Immanuel." A footnote with the word "woman" reads, "Or *virgin*." The King James Version translates Isaiah 7:14, "Therefore the Lord himself shall give you a sign; Behold, a virgin shall conceive, and bear a son, and shall call his name Immanuel."

The Revised Standard Version provides a translation that does not offend the Modernists who deny a supernatural God who foretells what he will do in the future. They also deny the virgin birth of the Lord Jesus Christ. This translation of Isaiah 7:14 is not a faithful witness to the text of what God has spoken by his Spirit through the prophet Isaiah centuries before the birth of Jesus. It obscures whether the Bible actually teaches that Jesus, who is Immanuel, God with us, was conceived supernaturally by the power of the Holy Spirit in the womb of the virgin Mary. The biblical teaching of the virgin birth of Jesus Christ is essential to the person and work of Christ. It is essential to the gospel of God's grace in Jesus Christ, which is the power of God unto salvation to everyone who believes. This translation of Isaiah 7:14 obscures the Biblical truth that Jesus Christ is the Son of God, who took upon himself man's nature so that he is "very God and very man, yet one Christ, the only Mediator between God and man" (WCF, 8.2), and therefore the only Savior of sinners.

When I was young, the New American Standard Bible was published as a revision of the American Standard Version of 1901, providing an alternative to the Revised Standard Version and also to the 1929 revision of the American Standard Version of 1901. Though highly acclaimed as a literal and accurate English translation, it is based on a critical text that follows the ideas of Westcott and Hort and favors questionable interpretations in the way it translates some prepositions and other words.

The New International Version of the Bible was published when I was growing up. Unlike the previous major English versions of the Bible, it was not a word-for-word translation, but rather sought faithfully to translate "the thought of the Biblical writers," frequently modifying sentence structure "with constant regard for the contextual meaning of words" (NIV, Preface). Like the Revised Standard Version and the New American Standard Bible, the New International Version was based on the critical text.

When I began to study Old Testament textual criticism in seminary, it became quite clear that the Lord had "by his singular care and providence kept pure in all ages" the Masoretic Text of the Hebrew Old Testament (WCF, 1.8). As I studied New Testament textual criticism in seminary, I found that the modern method of textual criticism, called eclecticism or rational criticism, is not based on biblical faith in the infinite, eternal, unchangeable, supernatural God, who created all things by the word of his power in the space of six days, and all very good, and reveals himself in his Word, which he breathed out and preserved.

Bruce M. Metzger describes the modern method of textual criticism as follows: "Consequently the editor of a text follows now one and now another set of witnesses in accord with what is deemed to be the author's style or the exigencies of transcriptional hazards" (*The Text of the New Testament*, 2nd. ed., 175). He continues:

> Another descriptive name which has been given to this procedure of handling the textual evidence is rational criticism. The use of the adjective 'rational' in this connexion is not intended to suggest that all other methods of criticism are irrational, but that the critic is concerned primarily with finding plausible reasons based on internal considerations

to justify in each case his choice of one reading as original and the others as secondary (176).

Metzger concludes, "By way of summary, it is obvious that there is much to commend the practice of judicious eclecticism in text criticism, for no one manuscript and no one family preserves the original text in its entirety." (178).

I also found Westcott and Hort's division of the Greek manuscripts into four types to be arbitrary and subjective, enabling them to impose their ideas on the text of Scripture rather than receiving the witness God has preserved. This led them to suggest only "probable" readings. Hort admits that textual criticism is:

... adopting at once in each case out of two or more variants that which looks most probable.... Internal Evidence of Readings is of two kinds, which cannot be too sharply distinguished from each other; appealing respectively to Intrinsic Probability, having reference to the author, and what may be called Transcriptional Probability, having reference to the copyists. In appealing to the first, we ask what an author is likely to have written: in appealing to the second, we ask what copyists are likely to have made him seem to write (Metzger, 129-130).

In addition, I found the rules provided by Metzger to guide the Pastor in the practice of modern textual criticism to lack sound judgment and thinking, not having an objective basis. Metzger himself admits:

Since textual criticism is an art as well as a science, it is understandable that in some cases different scholars will come to different evaluations of the significance of the evidence. This divergence is almost inevitable when, as sometimes happens, the evidence is so divided that, for example, the more difficult reading is found only in the later witnesses, or the longer reading is found only in the earlier witnesses (210).

By way of conclusion, let it be emphasized again that no single manuscript and no one group of manuscripts exists which the textual critic may follow mechanically. All known witnesses of the New Testament are to a greater or less extent mixed texts, and even the earliest manuscripts are not free from egregious errors. Although in very many cases the textual critic is able to ascertain without residual doubt which reading must have stood in the original, there are not a few other cases where he can only come to a tentative decision based on an equivocal balancing of probabilities. Occasionally none of the variant readings will commend itself as original, and he will be compelled either to choose the reading which he judges to be the least unsatisfactory or to indulge in conjectural emendation. In textual criticism, as in other areas of historical research, one must seek not only to learn what can be known, but also to become aware of what, because of conflicting witnesses, cannot be known (246).

The Greek New Testament published by the United Bible Societies uses the letters A, B, C, and D "to indicate the relative degree of certainty...for the reading adopted as the text. The letter A signifies that the text is virtually certain, while B indicates that there is some degree of doubt. The letter C means that there is a considerable degree of doubt whether the text or the apparatus contains the superior reading, while D shows that there is a very high degree of doubt concerning the reading selected for the text" (Introduction to *The Greek New Testament*, Third Corrected Edition, xii-xiii).

This stands in sharp contrast to the God who speaks in the Bible. He does not change and is unchangeable. There is no variableness, nor shadow of turning, with God. His promises in Christ are Yes and Amen. His Word is sure and cannot be broken. It is settled in heaven forever. "The supreme Judge, by which all controversies of religion are to be determined, and all decrees of councils, opinions of ancient writers, doctrines of men, and private spirits, are to be examined, and in whose sentence we are to rest, can be no other but the Holy Spirit speaking in the Scripture" (WCF, 1.10). We should have full persuasion and assurance of the infallible truth and divine authority of the Word of God, and we should have an infallible assurance of faith, founded upon the divine truth of the promises of salvation which God gives us in his Word (WCF, 1.5; 18.2).

The Bible teaches that the triune God is the primary author of Scripture, and he never makes a mistake. The triune God who speaks in Holy Scripture is more reliable than any person or any created thing here on earth. This triune God who speaks in Scripture has breathed out his infallible, inerrant, authoritative, perspicuous, and sufficient Word. In his Word he reveals himself to us, his creatures, made in his image to know, love, worship, and obey him. He has also preserved his Word in his singular care and providence and kept it pure in all ages so that we have the authentic Old Testament in Hebrew and the authentic New Testament in Greek. This is not at all like "other areas of historical research," as Metzger asserts.

The modern method of textual criticism focuses on the human authors and copyists of the Bible. When there are variant readings in the Greek New Testament, it suggests that each reader should make a rational guess about what a human author is likely to have written and whether it was accurately copied or was corrupted. This is fundamentally contrary to the biblical doctrine of God and his self-attesting revelation of himself to men. This undermines what we confess in the Westminster Confession of Faith, "The authority of the Holy Scripture, for which it ought to be believed, and obeyed, dependeth not upon the testimony of any man, or church; but wholly upon God (who is truth itself) the author thereof; and therefore it is to be received, because it is the Word of God" (WCF, 1.4).

The Lord blessed me with a New Testament professor in seminary who did not embrace the modern method of textual criticism and required his students to read several books by believing scholars who defended the proposition that the true New Testament text is found today in the majority of the Greek New Testament manuscripts, in the *Textus Receptus*, and in the King James Version and other faithful translations. Instead of arbitrarily dividing the Greek manuscripts of the New Testament into four principal types of texts, he taught that each manuscript is a witness that God has preserved to his Word and that the vast majority of manuscripts preserve the authentic New Testament text.

The oldest manuscripts are not necessarily the most accurate. They may, in fact, be the most inaccurate. God gave his Word to his church, and it is the responsibility of the church to be a faithful steward of that Word and to translate it into the common language of every nation. One of the means through which God has kept his Word pure through the centuries is the church faithfully preserving and making accurate copies of the Greek manuscripts. When an error was made in a manuscript, it was discarded. When a good manuscript wore out through use, another copy was carefully made of God's Holy Word. Similarly, when one's Bible wears out, he simply obtains another one (which is in no way less accurate than the old one).

The church of the Lord Jesus Christ should not neglect its duty to publish copies of both the Old Testament Hebrew text and the true New Testament Greek text, as well as faithful translations of each in the common language of every nation. Faithful ministers and believers should shine as lights in this dark world by holding forth that sure and pure Word of life so that the sound of the trumpet clearly warns men, women, and children to turn from their sins, believe in the only Savior of sinners, the Lord Jesus Christ, and have everlasting life. Only then can the church be the pillar and ground of the truth, the salt of the earth that has not lost its savor, and the light of the world that is like a city set on a hill that cannot be hidden.

Archibald A. Allison (B.A. Hillsdale College; M.Div. Theological College of the Canadian Reformed Churches and Bethel OPC) serves as Secretary of the Committee on Christian Education of the Orthodox Presbyterian Church, Secretary of the Board of Trustees of Great Commission Publications, Stated Clerk of the Presbytery of the Dakotas, and the Pastor of Emmaus OPC in Fort Collins, Colorado, where he resides with his wife and five children.

2

Is There Such a Thing as an Authentic Text?

Jonathan Arnold

One of the main distinctives of the Protestant Reformation was the doctrine of Scripture. The Roman Catholic Magisterium taught that only the church could properly interpret Scripture and was therefore the final authority for faith and practice. The traditional Protestant doctrine of Scripture as the sole authority for faith and practice attacks Roman Catholic doctrine at the root. Over recent decades a modernistic eclectic approach to Scripture has crept in and now seeks to replace both the Roman Catholic Magisterium and the classic Protestant doctrine of Scripture. In many ways, it has already succeeded.

An essential aspect of the Protestant doctrine of Scripture was the preservation of God's Word. The Westminster Confession states:

The Old Testament in Hebrew and the New Testament in Greek being immediately inspired by God, and, by His singular care and providence, kept pure in all ages, are therefore authentical; so as, in all controversies in religion, the church is finally to appeal unto them (WCF, 1.8).

The authenticity of God's Word—and its resulting integrity—is essential in establishing the Protestant doctrine of Scripture. On the other hand, if the Word of God has been corrupted through the centuries, this Protestant doctrine is in a precarious position.

The Roman Catholic Church grasped this early on and weaved into the Counter-Reformation the argument that variant readings in the Hebrew Old Testament and Greek New Testament rendered the scriptures' meaning uncertain. Therefore, the assessment and the verification of the scriptures falls to the Roman church. At the Council of Trent, they declared the Vulgate to be authentic "and that no one is to dare, or presume to reject it under any pretext whatever" (Trent, Fourth Session). The Protestant response is set out for us in various Reformed confessions such as the Westminster (1646), the Savoy (1658) and the Second London Baptist (1677/89). These confessions affirm that the verbal and plenary inspired Scripture, to which we have access in the present day, is the authentic, providentially preserved Hebrew Masoretic and Received Greek text.

If you believe in the verbal and plenary inspiration of the Hebrew Old Testament and Greek New Testament and believe that those scriptures are authentic—pure, true, and completely trustworthy—you also need to hold to the preservation of those scriptures. Many modern scholars think the traditional, preserved text is not fully authentic. Further, those who belong to the eclectic school of textual criticism see it as impossible to arrive at an authentic text. Bruce Metzger holds that,

> ...the text has suffered in transmission and that none of the versions provides a satisfactory restoration. Here we can only follow the best judgment of competent scholars as to the most probable reconstruction of the original text (*The Complete Parallel Bible*, 1993, xvi).

Modern textual critics believe that by comparing all the manuscripts and making changes to one word here and another word there we will progress to a better approximation of the original text, but not an authentic text. Evidently a large number of modern scholars (including those constructing the latest text for a Bible soon to be promoted to you) have the working assumption that we do not yet have the authentic text of Holy Scripture and never will.

This mistaken viewpoint should be a warning to all who regard the Word of God as authoritative and authentic. In order to hold to the providentially preserved scriptures kept pure in all ages (rather than more or less pure since the 1800s and subject to continuing updates), I adhere to the text that is commonly called the *Textus Receptus*. The acronym TR is given to the group of printed editions of the Greek New Testament made available in probably the greatest revival of truth Europe has ever seen: the Reformation. The TR is taken from the Greek texts which, for the most part, in the providence of God, were brought to Western Europe following the fall of Byzantium. The TR represents the majority of available Greek manuscripts (with a few notable exceptions).

2 Timothy 3:16 and 2 Peter 1:19-21 reveal that it is the written Scripture itself that is God-breathed, not just the doctrines or general teachings that flow from the written Word. All scripture—γραφή, the written word—is God-breathed. That being so, the very words of scripture are important, and if we are to have God's pure Word they need to be preserved as they have been given. As the Westminster and Second London Baptist Confessions of Faith state, the Old and New Testament texts kept pure in all ages "are therefore authentic; so as in all controversies of religion, the church is finally to appeal to them." Richard Muller observes:

> ...the Reformed orthodox insistence on the identification of the Hebrew and Greek texts as alone authentic does not demand direct reference to the *autographa* in those languages; the 'original and authentic text' of Scripture means, beyond the autograph copies, the legitimate tradition of Hebrew and Greek *apographa (Post-Reformation Reformed Dogmatics*, Vol. 2, 433).

This is important because it is in these "beyond the autograph copies," which are manifested in the printed TR editions, that the framers of the confessions had access to a reliable and authentic text.

Why Is the Text Used to Translate My Bible Important?

I first encountered the whole question of translation and text in my mid-teens while attending an evangelical conference in the United Kingdom. I was confronted during a meeting by one of the leaders who noticed I was reading a King James Version Bible. So shocked was he that he came up and told me in no uncertain terms that I should not be using that version—and proceeded to close my Bible and hand me the New International Version (the 1984 edition, the latest version at that time). It shook me. The KJV was the Bible my parents used. I had heard of many godly men in the vicinity of Westminster, such as Dr. Martyn Lloyd-Jones, who preached from it. What was the big issue here? In further conversations at the time I was told to trust the experts; more authentic manuscripts had been discovered, and therefore the KJV was just not reliable textually, and was not a good translation. I was also told I would understand this newer translation more easily. This is a story repeated in many other circumstances. The experts say we have found better manuscripts, so the person in the pew and the preacher in the pulpit embrace the new translations wholesale.

It is this sort of dynamic that has caused many to avoid the deep consideration of this topic that it deserves. To put one's head above the parapet and declare a TR position or even a preference for the KJV will have you branded an extremist by some. However, those who reject the TR without careful assessment fundamentally misunderstand our position and fail to grasp the connection between the prevailing reconstructionist views of the text of Scripture and the modern translations which they use. The incident I experienced caused me to be concerned about the whole topic, and to realize how important it is to know the text upon which my translation is based and why it is based on that text. The scriptures convinced me of the doctrine of providential preservation, as ably defended by men such as Turretin, Owen, and Keach.

The Principle of Theology

The reliability of the text of the Bible should be of fundamental concern to every Christian believer. In many systematic theology books, the doctrine of Scripture is placed in the first chapter. The whole substance and shape of the Christian faith depends on the words of the Bible. If we are basing our salvation on the premise that the holy scriptures are the Word of God, we must be concerned about its authenticity. Turretin states: "As the Word of God is the sole principle of theology, so the question concerning its necessity deservedly comes before all things" (*Institutes of Elenctic Theology*, "Holy Scriptures", Q1).

We also need to address the whole topic of the scriptures since there is a movement away from absolute truth which is chipping away at the edges of the theology of the true church and the Bible. Battles are being fought for key gospel doctrines and biblical living, but there has been a lack of attention to the foundation of our doctrine and practice: the Holy Bible.

In the Helvetic Consensus Formula, one of the issues they sought to counter was the influence of a textual critic named Cappellus who taught that both the vowel points and consonants of the Old Testament were corrupted (see Bowman, "A Forgotten Controversy," *Evangelical Quarterly*, 54; Muller, *After Calvin*, 151). In its third canon, this confession states:

Therefore, we are not able to approve of the opinion of

those who believe that the text which the Hebrew Original exhibits was de termined by man's will alone, and do not hesitate at all to remodel a Hebrew reading which they consider unsuitable, and amend it from the versions of the LXX and other Greek versions, the Samaritan Pentateuch, by the Chaldaic Targums, or even from other sources. They go even to the point of following the corrections that their own rational powers dictate from the various readings of the Hebrew Original itself which, they maintain, has been corrupted in various ways; and finally, they affirm that besides the Hebrew edition of the present time, there are in the versions of the ancient interpreters which differ from our Hebrew text, other Hebrew Originals. Since these versions are also indicative of ancient Hebrew Originals differing from each other, they thus bring the foundation of our faith and its sacred authority into perilous danger.

The same arguments made in this confessional statement can also be applied to the errors of contemporary textual criticism. The authoritative Word of God is at stake when we talk of the text of Scripture. Even if you are a skeptic regarding the TR position, I would urge you to consider the alternative and the necessary consequences of a text that is incomplete and that has been constantly subject to updates since the nineteenth century.

A Need to Retrace Our Steps

Alfred Martin warned in 1966 against textual critics and their theology when they move from collating and classifying to theorizing about the data assembled. He stated, "Christians who would not for a moment accept the leading of liberals in theology often unhesitatingly commit themselves to such leadership in New Testament textual criticism" ("John William Burgon—A Memorial", *Bibliotheca Sacra*, Vol. 123, 154). In another article noting the stand for truth taken by Edward Hills, Martin called for his generation not to take the wrong turn with Griesbach—a forefather of modern-day textual criticism—and to retrace their steps (*Sunday School Times*, Vol. 102, 116). May we also take up the challenge and call for a reassessment of the approach of orthodox believers to the Greek Text.

The Word's enduring quality derives from its divine origin, as does its resultant truth. It is truth of a special nature, truth applicable to men in all ages. God has given his Word to fallen sinners and thus revealed that he is merciful and gracious, able and willing to save sinners to the uttermost. Scripture itself informs us how perfection of communication was achieved: "All scripture is given by inspiration of God" (2 Timothy 3:16). The Holy Spirit so operated on the minds of the biblical writers that they wrote exactly what God intended. Inspiration extended to every word, so that "the Word of the Lord" meant a communication in which every word was from the Lord.

The doctrine of verbal inspiration has drawn many opponents since the German Enlightenment of the mid-eighteenth century. Out of that upheaval arose philosophers and theologians who made it their life work to challenge the orthodox doctrine of Scripture. The havoc they wrought has continued to the present day, as seen in the general acceptance of false theories regarding the nature of Scripture, and the substitution of false doctrines for true ones.

As many modern scholars support the assumption that we do not yet have the authentic text of Holy Scripture, they are not concerned with its very words. Sadly, this is even true of many evangelical scholars. To the evangelical believer, however, the authority of the Bible derives directly from God, every Word being so inspired that the whole Bible is literally the Word of God, and its preservation is essential, if he is to have access to the revealed truth of God. The Puritans and Reformers regarded Scripture as *autopistic* (i.e., that the scriptures are self-evidencing). The scriptures themselves determine to us what they are.

The Modern-day Problem

The problem faced by evangelical believers today is that the various extant ancient manuscripts of the Bible are not always identical. The available manuscripts of the Greek New Testament contain differences, many of which are minor, but some of which are significant. Further, the printed editions of the Greek text also differ among themselves, with some displaying the various reading options found in recently discovered manuscripts, such as that from the Vatican library. Faced with all these differences in the texts, the believer naturally should have a measure of concern. Many, however, simply delegate such discernment to the experts. Though it is indeed wise to receive instruction from Pastors, Elders, and scholars, each believer should also take the responsibility of personally understanding the current downgrade of Scripture.

The Greek New Testament is one of the most attested documents from the ancient world. There are over five thousand extant Greek manuscripts of the New Testament (i.e., in portions and books), and thousands of translations of it in other languages. The Reformers and Protestants of the sixteenth and seventeenth centuries did not rely on the statistics we have today, including recent manuscript discoveries. These kinds of statistics were not of chief concern to them, because they believed they had the authentic texts, as God's word endures forever and is kept pure in all ages (Isaiah 40:8; 1 Peter 1:24–25).

The Scriptures used by the Reformation titans of the faith are regarded by some Protestant scholars today as corrupted, filled with emendations and obscurities. Their view that Scripture is uncertain and ever-changing has led to a spirit of antagonism toward the doctrine of inspiration. We need to get back to a high view of Scripture, recognizing what is at stake if we abandon a providentially preserved Word. In the 1990s, there was a flourishing interest in the biblical view of creation. This proved a great blessing as the assumptions applied to scientific facts began to be viewed through the biblical worldview. The church needs a similar revival for the providentially preserved Word. We are not rejecting the evidence but are applying theological assumptions taught in the Bible to the Bible. This may appear to some as "circular reasoning," but the unconverted person will make the same charge against Christian faith in general.

The TR and Providential Preservation

In contrast to modern liberalism, the TR position recognizes the text that was used, for the most part, for centuries by Greek speaking Christians in the East, and then embedded in the Protestant churches during the Reformation. This was declared at the time in the confessions of faith as they affirmed the providentially preserved

Word of God. Benjamin Keach states regarding the Scriptures,

> ...there was but one Divine providence which over-ruled their various disclosures, and it was divinely ordered that their many books should finally be all united in one. To these astonishing miracles we may fitly add, the preservation of these holy writings for so many ages (*Troposchematologia*, viii-ix; cf. Book III, 59, 74).

There is a sad and distressing discrepancy in the very supposition that no exact superintending or peculiar providence has watched over the inspired books of Scripture and the text contained in those books. Some hold this unorthodox view, because there are competing manuscripts that contradict some parts of the text used by the church for centuries. We are told that due to the errors of copyists and translators there is no infallible text. So we now delegate to modern critics the task of discovering, distinguishing, and eliminating the human from the divine, and giving to the world and the church of today a new Bible.

The end result of this is the insinuation that the most devout expositors of the Holy Scriptures used an erroneous text, and that the church has not had access to the full, true scriptures. According to this reasoning, Calvin and Luther, Kiffin and Keach, Whitfield and Wesley did not have the correct scriptures. Further, we cannot say with any certainty that you and I, or our children, will ever have access to the true Bible in our lifetimes.

The King James Version of the Bible and those translations in other languages based on the Received Text are translations of God's

Word which we can publish and distribute in confidence, leaving it to the Lord to magnify his Word. The Lord has not placed the church on the uncertain ground of a yet-to-be established eclectic text. There is an authentic text. Those who desire the glory of God and edification of Christian brothers and sisters should strive to place Scripture in its proper place. The traditional or confessional text of the New Testament, known as the *Textus Receptus*, and its widely used printed edition produced by Scrivener, provide adequate access to what God has preserved. I urge you to consider the TR position and the consistency of maintaining a Word kept pure, and a reliable Bible for Christians at the time of the Reformation and today.

Jonathan D. Arnold (*studied at the London Reformed Baptist Seminary; LLB Hons. Open University, Milton Keynes) is the General Secretary of the Trinitarian Bible Society and is Pastor of Westminster Baptist Church in London, England, where he resides with his wife.*

3

God's Word as Creation - A Reason I Preach from the TR

Doug Barger

You have probably picked up this book because you are a Christian who desires to mature in your knowledge and understanding regarding a doctrine referred to as "Bibliology". Did you even know that you had a Bibliology? Well, you do, and it is one of the most fundamental and practical aspects of your Christian faith. Allow me to explain. Your doctrine of Bibliology provides answers to vital questions such as, "Is the Bible truly God's Word? What does it mean that the Bible is inspired? What books should comprise the Bible? What texts should we believe are God's Word? Does the Bible contain any errors, contradictions, or discrepancies?" Simply stated, your Bibliology is a summary of your beliefs regarding Holy Scripture and, as such, it is of paramount importance.

Now, let us just admit that for many of us, the answers to the questions above seem to be surrounded by technical and difficult issues that require laborious research and precious time, which very few of us who are raising families and faithfully supporting local churches have in excess. As a result, we tend simply to trust and rely on 'experts' and Bible publishers to settle these sorts of questions for us. I confess, this was the attitude I once held after my conversion to the Christian faith in 2001. In fact, it was not until I came under the teaching of Dr. Peter Masters while a student at the London Reformed Baptist Seminary (a ministry of Metropolitan Tabernacle Church) that I began to take my own Bibliology seriously. Afterwards, I began to serve as pastor of a church that subscribed to the Second London Baptist Confession of Faith, and was forced to deal with my Bibliology in light of this statement:

> The Old Testament in Hebrew (which was the native language of the people of God of old), and the New Testament in Greek (which at the time of the writing of it was most generally known to the nations), being immediately inspired by God, and by his singular care and providence kept pure in all ages (LBCF, 1.8; emphasis added).

It was the last phrase regarding being "kept pure in all ages" that I immediately perceived to be packed full of theological presuppositions. Thus, as was my custom, I wanted to dig a little deeper and ascertain what these heirs of the Reformation truly meant by such an assertion. More importantly, I had to answer the question: Am I convinced that their doctrinal formulations and underlying theology align with the teaching of Scripture? After all, this is what matters most (1 Thessalonians 5:21). As Andrew Fuller (1754-1815) wrote:

> The best criterion of a good system is its agreement with the Holy Scriptures. That view of things, whether we have any of us fully attained it or not, which admits the most natural meaning to be put upon every part of God's word, is the right system of religious truth (Andrew Fuller, *The Complete Works of Andrew Fuller, Memoirs, Sermons, etc.*, Vol. 1, 164).

After much study, and upon becoming satisfied with what I believed to be a clear understanding of their doctrine of Scripture, I found it to be the most convincing and reassuring expressions of faith in the canonical scriptures ever articulated by Christ's church.

As such, it served as a "criterion of a good system" in full agreement with "the Holy Scriptures" that aided me in the further development of my own Bibliology. In addition to how they dealt with textual issues, it was the pre-critical exegetical method of the framers, which demonstrated to me a refreshing contrast to what I had grown accustomed to hearing advocated by modern textual critics. These modern scholars articulated an altogether different interpretive method and view of Scripture.

This, among other reasons, led me to believe that the covenant keeping God of all creation, in an act of special grace toward his elect and general benevolence unto all mankind, preserved all his Word in what is commonly referred to as the Masoretic Text of the Hebrew Old Testament and the Received Text of the Greek New Testament. My goal in contributing to this book is to aid you in the development of your own Bibliology, with the aim that you too will not only agree with the earlier assertion of the LBCF, but also other historic theologians of the past such as John Gill (1697-1771), who affirmed in similar fashion, "The Scriptures are the words of God; and they are pure and holy, free from all human mixtures, and from all fraud and deceit; they are the Scriptures of truth" (*An Exposition of the Old Testament*, Psalm 12:6).

An approach to this whole issue which has helped me arrive at a place where I can fully agree with the above sentiments of the venerable Dr. Gill is rather straightforward and simple. I admit that it is not unique to me, but rather one which I have repeatedly observed, either explicitly or implicitly, in the written works of eminent men from prior centuries within the Reformed, Presbyterian, Congregationalist, and Baptist traditions. This approach is, namely, that in the formulation of their Bibliology they insisted firstly that one must possess a clear understanding of Scripture's unique role within creation, and secondly appreciate fully the interest which the Father, Son, and Spirit maintain regarding Scripture's created purpose. I told you it was simple and straightforward: Scripture's unique role as something God created with distinct purpose. This simple analysis must inform one's beliefs about the nature and reliability of Holy Scripture. When thoughtfully employed, this model establishes an objective foundation upon which to evaluate accurately the various claims seeking to influence our beliefs. No matter where the claims originate, one must always ask, "Do these claims align with what I know to be true regarding the uniquely created role of Scripture and God's purpose for it?"

Let us here take a step back and first recognize that what we are initially considering is (at its most fundamental level) God's purpose in creating Scripture. The inspired Word of God is then a part of creation. As such,

> God the good creator of all things, in His infinite power and wisdom, doth uphold, direct, dispose, and govern all creatures and things, from the greatest even to the least, by His most wise and holy providence, *to the end for which they were created*, according unto His infallible foreknowledge, and the free and immutable counsel of His own will; to the praise of the glory of His wisdom, power, justice, infinite goodness, and mercy (LBCF, 5:1; Hebrews 1:3; Job 38:11; Isaiah 46:10,11; Psalm 135:6; Matthew 10:29-31; Ephesians 1:11; emphasis added).

In one sense, the Triune God's ultimate end in the creation of Scripture is the gathering and perfecting of a glorious church, without spot, wrinkle, holy and without blemish (Ephesians 5:27). From their initial creation, God's written words began to move all redemptive history toward this end, while the rest of creation, as the Puritans were fond of saying, was simply 'a window dressing for the church'.

Stop and think about that. The Creator God chose to condescend to us as mere men and communicate with us through his own words! It was God himself who inspired men like Moses, Solomon, Paul, and John to write his words on media appropriate for their times, such as papyrus, animal skins, etc. (2 Peter 1:21). This was necessary, because nothing else in all of creation could accomplish such a task of expressing the fullest perfections and purposes of a transcendent, infinite God unto created, finite man. As Abraham Booth (1734-1806) observes:

> ...though the existence of a Supreme Being may be clearly seen by the things that are made, even his eternal power and Godhead; yet the circumstances of mankind have ever been such, as to render it necessary that a more positive and explicit revelation of the perfections and purposes, of the works and ways of the great Creator, should be given to them (Abraham Booth, *The Works of Abraham Booth*, Vols. 1-3, Vol. 1, 28).

Holy Scripture, as this positive and explicit revelation, serves as the infallible test of all things. As the prophet warns, "To the law and to the testimony: if they speak not according to this word, it is because there is no light in them" (Isaiah 8:20). Likewise, Jesus emphasizes this role of Scripture when he instructs us to "Search the Scriptures" (John 5:39). Why? Because Holy Scripture is the ultimate standard for all things.

It may go without saying that such a standard, once admitted, would require maintenance to ensure its purity from corruption (lest it be deprived of its authority). If Scripture's created role was jeopardized, it could not serve perpetually as the one and only trusted standard, accurately reflecting the perfect wisdom and will of God. We can be certain that the maintenance and preservation of this purity has been performed by God himself throughout history, if for no other reason than to preserve the Scriptures' usefulness in revealing his authority within his created economy.

If one was to suggest that only some parts of God's Word, endowed as it is with such a noble role in creation, have been purely preserved by God, and at the same time maintain that other parts of his inscribed Word have not been upheld in purity by his same providence, he has, in effect, called into question the very wisdom and power of God. This suggestion would be wholly inconsistent with the biblical revelation that through his written word, God has provided his church everything which is profitable for doctrine, for reproof, for correction, for instruction in righteousness: that the church may be perfect, thoroughly furnished unto all good works (2 Timothy 3:16). Recall from Ephesians 5:27 the "ultimate end" of God's Word. Thus, in his inspired words, he has provided us a "certain way" and a "certain rule". To suggest otherwise would be contrary to all we know of God. Consider how Benjamin Keach (1640-1704) conveys this thought:

> If the Holy Scriptures be not the certain way and means of faith and practice, or of faith and repentance, then God hath left us no certain rule or means. And be sure this cannot stand consistent with the wisdom, goodness, mercy, honor and faithfulness of the holy God (Benjamin Keach, *The Scriptures Superior to All Spiritual Manifestations*, 303-304).

Keach brings up an important point here: Which Bibliology is most "consistent with the wisdom, goodness, mercy, honor, and faithfulness of the holy God" (especially in view of the role God intends for his written Word in creation)?

One answer could be: A Bibliology which is convinced that God decreed human error would corrupt his written word, and did so to such a degree that his people have little hope of ever possessing it free from errors. A better answer would be: A Bibliology which by faith is convinced that God has specially kept his written word pure from human error, and thus his people can say yes and amen to its witness with certainty, unto the glory of God.

As a husband, father, and pastor of a local church, I am persuaded that it is of the greatest importance for my family and the church to receive genuine profit from the written Word of God. They must, by God's grace, become convinced that the *creator* of Scripture is also the absolute protector of Scripture. If the authority and purity of Scripture is not reliable and compelling, then I have no basis to point them to it as the foundation of their faith and obedience. This, I trust, strikes the conscience of every thoughtful Christian husband, father, or church leader.

Do you believe that God has protected his word from mixture and human error throughout history? One of the most eminent scholars of Scripture and defenders of Christian orthodoxy most certainly did:

The wonderful preservation of them [scriptures], through all the changes and declensions of the Jewish church and state, to whom the books of the Old Testament were committed; and notwithstanding the violence and malice of Heathen persecutors, particularly Dioclesian, who sought to destroy every copy of the Scriptures, and published an edict for that purpose, and notwithstanding the numbers of heretics, and who have been in power, as also the apostasy of the church of Rome; and yet these writings have been preserved, and kept pure and incorrupt... to which may be subjoined the testimony of God himself (John Gill, *An Exposition of the New Testament*, 2 Timothy 3:16).

The purity of God's words within creation is a testimony of God himself unto his creation. Meditate upon that for a minute or two. I assure you, doing so will mature and develop your Bibliology.

In closing, imagine if you and I were standing at the foot of Mount Sinai when Moses descended from on high with the two inscribed tables of stone, written on either side by the finger of God. No doubt, we would have been overwhelmed by such an extraordinary event. Further, I speculate that we would have been among those who desired carefully to examine their letters, their words, indeed, every peculiar circumstance related to such a divinely created monument, conveying the power and authority of God. If so, we would have received it, guarded it, and carefully transmitted it, with respect to its purpose and form.

Our God, who inscribed those tablets of stone on that climatic day is the one and same God who, through plenary inspiration, has given us his very words throughout the ages. Just as he by his singular care and providence kept the ten commandments pure in all ages, we can be assured that he has done so with all Scripture. Why do I make the decision to lead my family and the local church using a Bible that utilizes the Masoretic Text in Hebrew and Received Text in Greek? In part, it is because I am convinced that God has appointed his Word for a special use in creation. This use has never changed, so God continues with special interest to guard its purity.

So then, you have a choice to make regarding your own Bibliology. Do you accept the current claims of the modern "textual critics" who suggest that God has permitted human error to corrupt his inspired words? Lacking positive proof and offering theories which are often nothing more than unverifiable conjectures, such scholars nevertheless convince many that the Bible contains words, phrases, and entire passages that are not inspired. They teach that since the scriptures were not maintained by God and kept pure, we now possess Bibles that perpetuate impurities and errors.

Will your Bibliology (i.e., your beliefs about God and his Word), accept such unverifiable conjectures? Or will you rather, through eyes of faith, see God's hidden hand at work in history, as demonstrated by his zealous protection of his inspired words? Because he himself is pure, he keeps his every word, and thus we love both God and his word (Psalm 119:140). Those who believe that God has indeed preserved and protected his inspired words ought to welcome discussions that relate to the history of how our faithful, covenant-keeping God has delivered this gift to us. At the same time, we should also, in a spirit of gentleness and meekness, seek to point people away from the presumptions of the modern critics to the testimony of God himself.

Doug Barger (B.A. International Business College; Dipl. Business Management Ivy Tech University, student at London Reformed Baptist Seminary) is founder of Particular Baptist Heritage Books and serves as Pastor of Christ Reformed Baptist Church in New Castle, Indiana, where he resides with his wife and three children.

4

From Atheism to the Authorized Version

Gavin Beers

The Apostle Paul, when describing his conversion to faith in Christ, wrote to Timothy that he, "was before a blasphemer, and a persecutor, and injurious" (1 Timothy 1:13). I was all these things myself. In my case, I was a child of the Church who rejected the faith and became something of an evangelist for my new found atheism, never missing an opportunity to mock the gospel of Christ and those who adhered to it. But like Saul of Tarsus "I obtained mercy," and learned "that Christ Jesus came into the world to save the chief of sinners" (v. 15).

Though I had been a child of the Church for fifteen years, sadly I was biblically ignorant. That, in itself, is not uncommon, but it was not just that I did not understand the Bible, I did not know any of it. True, I knew the general contours of a few Old Testament stories or

New Testament parables that were discussed in my Sunday School classes, but I did not know the texts themselves, and while I heard many things about Jesus and what he did, I had no understanding of *why* he did any of it.

The Bible I read as a child was "The Good News Bible" and my sole memory of it is that it is distinctly unmemorable. The only verses of Scripture I recall from my childhood are those placarded on telegraph poles and farmhouses across my home country of Northern Ireland, texts like John 3:16—"For God so loved the world, that he gave his only begotten Son, that whosoever believeth in him should not perish, but have everlasting life." All of these were from a different, much older, but yet more memorable translation: The Authorized or King James Version of the Bible.

I was converted to faith in Christ at the age of twenty when I went with a friend's father to a local congregation of the Free Presbyterian Church of Ulster. It was a denomination very different from the one I had grown up in and remains a unique blend of an older Irish Presbyterianism and American Fundamentalism. One thing that was obvious to me from the beginning was their commitment to the King James Version of the Bible, which naturally became my Bible.

Some people would view the context of my conversion and conclude that it was the fundamentalist and not the Reformed component of my church environment that made me an adherent of the King James Version. In the beginning, I admit that this may have been the case. The rhetoric was at times very powerful and sometimes not particularly well articulated, but it was enough to make a young Christian at least think he knew what he was talking about. After some time, however, my developing biblical convictions took me away from that more 'fundamentalist' way of thinking, and toward a more consciously Reformed and Confessional approach to the Christian Faith. Many of my perspectives changed on issues like the Regulative Principle of Worship and evangelism methodology, but one thing that remained the same was a commitment to the Authorized Version. This deepened through my seminary training both in Northern Ireland and in Scotland, where I was exposed to more concentrated study of the issues involved, and my conviction came to rest simply and firmly upon two great pillars. The first is *theological* and the second *textual*, and the theological informs how I understand the textual.

The Theological Pillar

Special Revelation from God is necessary with respect to fallen men to address our need as sinners. God has graciously met that need by revealing in Scripture both himself and his will for our salvation. All Scripture is given by inspiration of God (2 Timothy 3:16) and is an all-sufficient rule for our faith and practice. God did not merely reveal and donate his Word in a general way but in a particular manner to his Church (Psalm 147:19-20; Romans 3:1-2; Ephesians 1:1; Philippians 1:1). Further, God has promised to preserve the precious Word that he inspired in its entirety, so that it will not be lost to the Church in the world. The above truths are confessed in the Westminster Confession of Faith chapter 1, and of particular note are words in paragraph 8 (emphasis added):

The Old Testament in Hebrew (which was the native language of the people of God of old), and the New Testament in Greek (which, at the time of the writing of it was most generally known to the nations), *being immediately inspired by God, and, by his singular care and providence, kept pure in all ages, are therefore authentical*; so as, in all controversies of religion, the Church is finally to appeal unto them. But, because these original tongues are not known to all the people of God, who have right unto and interest in the Scriptures, and are commanded, in the fear of God, to read and search them, *therefore they are to be translated into the vulgar language of every nation* unto which they come, that the Word of God dwelling plentifully in all, they may worship Him in an acceptable manner; and, through patience and comfort of the Scriptures, may have hope.

While it is the original autographs alone that are inspired, and these have all been lost to the Church for centuries, God has promised to preserve pure that inspired Word by his singular care and providence. If this were not so, we could have no confidence whatsoever that we have the Word of God. This providential preservation poses no problem to the infinite God who governs all things in the history of the created universe by that same holy, wise, and powerful providence. Therefore, we are to understand and expect that, in this way, God has superintended the process of copying the original autographs and the manuscripts that developed from them in the Church, to preserve his Word in the world.

This theology directs us to look for certain things in a translation of the Bible. It will be the best and most accurate translation we have in our own language of the text or manuscript tradition that God has providentially preserved in and has been used by the Church. All of these components are important—the Inspirational, the Providential, the Ecclesiastical. God did not donate or reveal his Word into the hands of a group of random secular academics, but he gave it to his Church. Nor did he transfer the rights to the Bible to a host of profit-motivated publishing companies to proliferate countless numbers of translations. We are looking for a translation of the inspired Word of God from a preserved and ecclesiastical text.

The Textual Pillar

So where are we to find and identify that text? As you might expect when you consider the history of the Church, there were multitudes of manuscripts copied, produced, and circulated in the early Church. These were often copied with painstaking care and oversight, yet human fallibility also led to the existence of scribal errors and im-perfections. Through time, certain families of texts developed (e.g., the Byzantine, Alexandrian, and Caesarean texts), all of which were characterized either by additions or omissions depending on which one is taken to be the standard.

Keeping within our theological parameters above, however, we are looking for a text in the original languages that has been preserved and used consistently in the Church throughout the centuries. History reveals a predominance of the Byzantine family of texts which supply us with the majority of extant manuscripts in the Church. The Latin Vulgate originally followed and was revised to conform with the Byzantine tradition and at the Reformation, the Protestant Church generally followed this family of texts, and it was compiled into the "Received Text" by Erasmus in his printed work from 1516. This was the basis for Martin Luther's original translation of the Bible into German (1522); William Tyndale's translation of the New Testament into English (1525); The Coverdale Bible (1535); The Matthew Bible (1537); The Great Bible (1539); The Geneva Bible (1560); The Bishops' Bible (1568); and the Authorized or King James Version (1611).

The King James Bible was the standard English translation used in churches from the seventeenth to the nineteenth centuries. Then, with the discovery of older manuscripts in the nineteenth century, textual critics were motivated to produce new, reconstructed editions of the Greek New Testament. These texts, which are significantly different from the Received Text, became the basis for the many of the modern English translations we have today. If the doctrine of providential preservation is true, why would we employ manuscripts that appear to have been lost to the Church for centuries to correct the textual tradition that had been preserved and received? Furthermore, why would we adopt an eclectic approach to textual reconstruction that is evolutionary in principle (i.e., an approach that is open ended, leaving the text in a state of perpetual emendation in accordance with the latest discoveries)? Revealed theology must here take precedence over the argument of antiquity (i.e., just because a text is deemed to be old does not mean that it is more accurate). We are looking for a text that has been preserved and used in the Church, not just a text that is old.

A man could spend a few lifetimes looking into all the articles and arguments written on the subject of biblical textual criticism, and I am appreciative of the labor that many have expended there.

For me, the question remains quite simple: What is the most accurate English translation of the preserved and ecclesiastically received biblical text? In my opinion, the answer at present is clearly the Authorized or King James Version of the Bible. This is why I read and preach from it.

Personal Considerations

I find the theological and textual arguments compelling for the use of the Authorized Version. They carry the ultimate weight forming my practice, but I would also like to add a few observations that are more personal. In particular, I wish to address one of the more common criticisms of the King James Version of the Bible: that its archaic language is not fitted for use in the twenty-first century, as it poses a hindrance to our presentation of the gospel.

I have heard this many times and watched as churches have changed to Bible translations based on the modern eclectic text. In over two decades as a Christian and fifteen years in the ministry, however, I have found this to be much more of a projected than real problem. I was a child of the late twentieth century, science-minded, and certainly not literary in my tastes. I was the kind of person for whom the Church is supposed to have to change her Bible version. Yet, contrary to popular myth, the use of the King James Bible posed no problem to me. I have found the same in my ministry working among the old and young, the educated and the uneducated, those inside the Church and those outside the Church. The use of the King James Bible has never posed a problem.

I do have other versions of the Scriptures in my library, and I consult them from time to time. I have, on a few occasions, thought to read through one of these in my personal devotions, as have other members of my family. The result has always been the same. Within a few weeks I migrate back to the King James Version. I am compelled theologically and textually to rest there, and I am content personally to remain there until such times as a better, more accurate translation of the Received Text may be produced in the future.

Gavin Beers (Dipl. Free Church Seminary) is the Pastor of Cornerstone Presbyterian Church, North American Presbytery of the Free Church (Continuing) in Burlington, North Carolina, where he resides with his wife and six children.

5

The Text of the Church

Poul de Gier

What does the Received Text have to do with a bi-vocational Pastor and dairy farmer living in a rural community? What led a small confessionally Reformed Baptist Church to embrace a Bible based on the Received Text for its ministry?

Being an immigrant child from the Netherlands, I experienced first-hand the reality of translating languages. Words do not always translate well, and some words do not even exist in the other language, so it is no wonder that translating the Bible from the original languages is difficult. For years I used the New International Version, and then a friend of mine switched to the King James Version. I was around seventeen years old and vividly remember telling my parents how I would go visit him and set him straight. I came home with a book. That changed everything. Up to that time, I thought the debate was simply a matter of translation philosophy (i.e., literal word-for-word versus translating thought-for-thought). I then learned that the bigger question to be asked before how to translate is what to translate. I discovered that a big change had taken place in the *what* (i.e., Bibles are translated from *different* texts of the original languages). It is here where the discussion must first take place. The methodology and presuppositions embraced with respect to text will lead to completely different foundations, and ultimately, different Bibles.

What's in question?

People somewhat familiar with this issue will be aware of the "biggies": Mark 16:9-20, the *Pericope Adulterae* (John 7:53-8:11), and the *Comma Johanneum* (1 John 5:7-8). But what most people do not realize is that there are *many more* differences. When one actually examines the differences, they will see the list is quite large (cf. *Textual Key to the New Testament: A List of Omissions and Changes*, available from the Trinitarian Bible Society). Most people do not take the time to look at the differences. Instead, they simply repeat the worn axiom, "No doctrine of Scripture is changed." I am always surprised by this statement, especially when heard from Reformed brothers. We love the Word. We preach the Word. We carefully and prayerfully exegete passages and study the original languages. Theological nuances are determined by *the words*. Are the changes in wording then trivial as long as a doctrine is mentioned at least *somewhere* else? I cannot say that I am comfortable with that argument. Whether or not the doctrine can be found elsewhere, if God inspired it, then it is part of his Word.

The more I studied the issue, the more I realized that the modern view of Scripture is a departure from the confessional view. Our Reformed forebearers understood plenary inspiration and preservation as two sides of the same coin. Both the Westminster and London Baptist Confessions affirm that the Holy Scriptures, "being immediately inspired by God, and by his singular care and providence kept pure in all ages, are therefore authentic" (WCF & LBCF, 1.8).

The Modern View

What changed? The meaning of preservation. Whereas the Church historically believed that the scriptures had been preserved through God's providence in the actual use of the church, the modern view deemed the text so lost, or corrupted, that it was in need of restoration. This new view is reflected in the doctrinal statements of many churches and seminaries. Many assign the infallibility and inerrancy of the Bible only to "the originals", which no one has. Since the original text was supposedly lost, the textual critics (many of whom are not orthodox believers) take on the task of "restoring" them. How confident can we be that they are doing a good job? By employing an Enlightenment philosophy of "pure reason" they never stop tinkering with the text. It is never-settled, always shifting. The following two reasons are commonly given:

Reason One:
"Older and better manuscripts have been discovered."

To engage this argument is to allow the restorationist worldview. It requires an admission that the Bible has been lost and needs to be restored. Even for those who embrace this line of thinking, the water gets pretty murky. The two most popular "older and better" manuscripts (*Vaticanus* and *Sinaiticus*) are full of corrections, deletions, contradictions, and questionable markings. Furthermore, there are so few ancient *papyri* that they can hardly be given the weight often attributed to them. All we can really say about older manuscripts is just that: they are older.

Reason Two:

"We have more manuscripts now than ever before."

It is true that we possess over 5,000 Greek manuscripts of the New Testament. What is not often acknowledged is how fragmentary many of the earliest of these manuscripts are. Many contain just portions of New Testament books. Very few are complete. To the defender of the modern view, this appears as no problem. As explained by James White in a debate with Bart Ehrman in 2009, "There is every reason to believe that our problem is not having 95% of what was originally written, but instead, of having 101%. As Rob Bowman has put it, it is like having a 1,000-piece jigsaw puzzle, but you have 1,010 pieces in the box. The task is weeding out the extra; the originals are there." This analogy, while clever, is unconvincing. How does one know the puzzle contains 1,000 pieces? One does not have the original box! It could be a 900 piece puzzle or a 1,200 piece puzzle, so how do you know? This is precisely what you are trying to determine!

Furthermore, another rarely mentioned fact is how many manuscripts have disappeared since the time the first printed Bibles were produced. Many have been lost in wars, fires, and theft. This means there are a lot of missing manuscripts which were available when the Bible was first printed. This also means our best authority is not the currently extant manuscripts, but what the faithful church has received!

Some appeal to the totality of the manuscript evidence, but in which era? From what point in history is this "totality" measured? As new theories are proposed, new texts get printed. The text of the Bible is never settled and always open to tinkering. To quote a leading text critic from our day,

> Do we have a reliable text of the New Testament? Are there places where the Bible misquotes Jesus? The short answer is there is no way to tell. We don't have the originals, or the original copies, or copies of the copies. There are passages that scholars continue to debate, is this the original text or not? And there are some passages where we will never know the answer (Bart Ehrman, *Did the Bible Misquote Jesus?* 2009 debate).

The Confessional View

The confessional view of the text of Scripture begins with theology. That is, what does God's Word say about itself regarding preservation? Consider the following passages: Psalm 12:6-7, "The words of the LORD are pure words: as silver tried in a furnace of earth, purified seven times. Thou shalt keep them, O LORD, thou shalt preserve them from this generation for ever." Matthew 5:18, "For verily I say unto you, Till heaven and earth pass, one jot or one tittle shall in no wise pass from the law, till all be fulfilled." Matthew 24:35, "Heaven and earth shall pass away, but my words shall not pass away."

These verses (and more) testify that the Bible, as inspired, will also be preserved. Paul also makes clear that the scriptures would be available for the church, writing, "For whatsoever things were written aforetime were written for our learning, that we through patience and comfort of the scriptures might have hope" (Romans 15:4) and "All scripture is given by inspiration of God, and is profitable for doctrine, for reproof, for correction, for instruction in righteousness"(2 Timothy 3:16). The Scriptures must be available to every generation; otherwise, how could its promised profitability be actualized? How could we be held accountable to its message, if the message itself is in question? How could the Church appeal to Scripture as her authority when the authority has been lost? The doctrine of preservation is a vital consequence of the doctrine of inspiration.

The Bible itself teaches that God himself preserves the scriptures by means of his covenant people. Paul writes of the Jews that "unto them were committed the oracles of God" (Romans 3:2), establishing that they were the custodians of the Old Testament. The New Covenant community, the Church, was similarly appointed as the custodian of Scripture in the New Covenant age. The Church is "the pillar and ground of the truth" (1 Timothy 3:15), which is to preserve, defend, and transmit the scriptures for future generations.

Just as the early Christians received and carefully transmitted the apostolic preaching, so also did they receive and carefully transmit the apostolic writings (cf. 1 Thessalonians 2:13; 1 Corinthians

15:1-4). This means that the Word of God is organically preserved in orthodox churches through faithful preaching of the gospel and glad reception of the scriptures. Thus, we should not expect apostate churches, heretical teachers, or unbelieving scholars to be trustworthy in their teaching or transmission of the scriptures. Though individual believers may embrace compromised texts, the Church will organically reject corrupted scriptures and preserve the Word of God. Thus, the scriptures will be available in every generation, even though there may be regions where it is not completely available, due to corruption, persecution, or the absence of faithful churches.

In addition to its theological basis, the confessional view of the text of Scripture may also be supported by a consideration of history. From the beginning of the Church, the Apostles warned the saints about false teachers who would attempt not only to corrupt the message of Scripture, but also the scriptures themselves (2 Peter 3:15-16). Early heretics tampered with the scriptures and entire regions, such as Egypt, were affected. Thus, differences in the early manuscript record are unsurprising. Early manuscripts often show mixed readings from various manuscript families, demonstrating that early alterations were not uniform.

Eventually, by the seventh century, the Western churches abandoned the Greek text altogether and adopted the Latin Vulgate. The Eastern Byzantine Empire, however, retained the Greek language and the Greek biblical manuscripts. These manuscripts represented the voices of hundreds of unique witnesses from a wide geographical distribution. They spoke in concert of the text of Scripture in actual use. By the end of the first millennium, the Byzantine text was dominant, most other textual streams being rejected or falling into disuse. Four events then coalesced providentially to bring this dominant text into print. First, Gutenberg invented the printing press around 1436. Second, there was the Fall of Constantinople in 1453, which caused many manuscripts to be carried by refugees into western Europe. Third, the "Renaissance" movement promoted the return "to the sources" [*ad fontes*] in their original languages, thus reviving Greek and Hebrew studies. Fourth, the Protestant Reformation began in 1517 with the posting of Martin Luther's Ninety-five Theses.

After the printing press was invented, hand copying died out as the Bible could now be mass-produced. Pious men like Jacob ben Chayyim brought the Hebrew Masoretic text to print, while devout scholars such as Erasmus and Beza edited the manuscripts of the Greek New Testament. Only those living at that time could speak with authority about how many manuscripts were actually available to them. These manuscripts needed editing to identify scribal mistakes, but such editing principally functioned from the believing presupposition, "We have the Bible." Instead of marginalizing the actual use of the Bible through church history, it emphasized it. The Westminster divines "were fully aware that this providential preservation was not to be confined to one copy, but applied to the manuscripts and codices which were extant in their own day, *and had been in continual use in the church*" (Garnet Howard Milne, *Has the Bible Been Kept Pure?*, 204; emphasis added).

By the time the major Reformed confessions were being written, the standard text had been affirmed, even in places where there were significant variants. For example, regarding 1 John 5:7, Francis

Turretin wrote "...for although some formerly called it into question and heretics now do, yet all the Greek copies have it, as Sixtus Sensis acknowledges: 'they have been the words of never-doubted truth, and contained in all the Greek copies from the very times of the apostles.' (*Bibliotheca sancta*, 1575, 2:298)" (Francis Turretin, *Institutes of Elenctic Theology*, Vol. I, 115). Two eminent textual scholars of the twentieth century also make the following admissions:

> It is undisputed that from the 16th to the 18th century orthodoxy's doctrine of verbal inspiration assumed this *Textus Receptus*. It was the only Greek text they knew, and they regarded it as the "original text" (Kurt Aland, "The Text Of The Church?", *Trinity Journal*, 8 (Fall 1987): 132).

> **The *Textus Receptus* is the text of the Church**. It is that form of text which represents the sum total and the end product of all the textual decisions which were made by the Church and her Fathers over a period of more than a thousand years (Merrill M. Parvis, as cited in F. N. Jones, *Which Version is the Bible?*, 207).

Challenges in Ministry

It was these convictions that led our church to use the Received Text. The leadership spent a winter studying the New King James Version for potential use in the pulpit but felt retaining the KJV was more beneficial. For example, the more one understands the intentionality of the "thees" and "thous," the "-ests" and "-eths," the more one appreciates how well the translators captured the nuances of the original text. Has maintaining this position always been easy? No. It is not a majority position, and the KJV is not colloquial English. Have some misunderstood our church because of our position? Probably. Some might even think we are "King James Only", but we consider that a dangerous position to hold.

A few years ago, our church leadership was studying a book in which one contributor spilled a lot of ink on a particular textual variant. We all walked away realizing that in the modern view each person becomes his own "Bible-builder." The "experts" admit this with regular usage of words like: "probably," "seemingly," "possibly," or "likely." Imagine preaching like that! Our faith demands that "we have a more sure word" (2 Peter 1:19), and we have it in the Word of God, inspired, preserved, and kept pure in all ages.

Poul de Gier (B.Sc. The King's University of Edmonton) is an Elder and main teacher/preacher at Grace Fellowship Church in Ponoka, Alberta, Canada, where he resides on a dairy farm with his wife and four children.

6

Promise and Faith

Tanner Dikin

The subject of identifying the authentic text of scripture is one for which I have a lot of affection. It is a part of the faith that I have been interested in most of my life, so I am very thankful for the opportunity to contribute to this anthology of essays. I pray God's blessing on it.

Undoubtedly, you have already read essays in this volume explaining the modern theory of textual criticism, so I will not belabor those points. For the sake of brevity, I have separated this essay into three headings describing my own personal experience. First, in the biographical section, I will share how I started believing in the authenticity of the Received Text. In the doctrinal section, I will explain how I came to think about Scripture. Finally, in the practical section, I will testify as to how the theology of the text has helped our church.

Biographical: Coming to the Text

When I was first asked to contribute to this book, I was afraid that all I would be able to say was, "I've held to this position all my life" since my parents and grandparents imparted their skepticism of modern Bible translations to me at an early age. I remember when my mother took me to buy my first children's Bible. I had my eyes set on a grownup looking leather one. I picked it up, and she lovingly told me it was the wrong kind and said I needed one with the letters 'KJV' on the side. I came home with a colorful 'Read to Me' Bible. That was my first memory learning about different translations of the Bible. Some might say that my confidence in the Received Text is just childhood hetero-suggestion from my family, but I prefer not to use psychological categories. We should recognize that Proverbs 22:6 correctly says, "Train up a child in the way he should go: and when he is old, he will not depart from it."

This is not to say that I never questioned the reliability of the Received Text. In high-school, I started preparing for the ministry of preaching. My youth Pastor met with me once a week with the intention of teaching me about doctrine and the work of ministry. At one point, he told the youth group about the Septuagint (a flawed Greek translation of the Old Testament) and concluded that our translations were also errant. He tried to persuade me to drop the KJV, but I stuck it out and even persuaded my friend to start using the Authorized Version as well. That minister eventually hinted that he did not want to meet with me anymore, and that was that. That episode stuck with me for some time, and I wrestled with whether or not I could reasonably continue to prefer the KJV.

Doctrinal: Settled in the Text

The unease I felt about my heritage was eventually settled after I moved to a church closer to where I lived, and started seriously studying the topic. I went through three stages in my development towards the confessional text position: biblical, theological, and historical.

My first step was learning what the Bible said about itself. There are many places where the Word of God claims preservation. For example, Matthew 5:18 reads, "For verily I say unto you, till heaven and earth pass, one jot or one tittle shall in no wise pass from the law, till all be fulfilled." Christ here claims that the scriptures will stand, as given, until the end of the world. He even applies this truth to the letters which constitute the text of Scripture. It is noteworthy that he says this in the context of the practical use of the scripture. In verse 19, he points out that the use of the law for teaching must be consistent with the practice of the teacher, saying "Whosoever shall do and teach them, the same shall be called great in the kingdom of heaven." So the preservation of scripture is not a vague statement of fact, disengaged from personal application. It is a truth that I may know for myself, by consistently applying it to my Christian walk.

Another passage which affirms the preservation of scripture is Psalm 12:6-7, "The words of the LORD are pure words: as silver tried in a furnace of earth, purified seven times. Thou shalt keep them, O LORD, thou shalt preserve them from this generation for ever." In this Psalm, God promises to guard, and liberate his people from corrupt rulers. To this end, he says "Now will I arise... I will set him in safety..." (v. 5). This is partly what vv. 6-7 addresses. Not only is the Word of God called "pure... purified," but it also intimates that God will "preserve" and "keep" both his people and these "pure" words of promise.

There are also points of theological reflection which make little sense unless we recognize the work of God in preserving the Scripture. One such point is the doctrine of the Church. In Ephesians 2:20 we read that we, as the Church, "are built upon the foundation of the apostles and prophets, Jesus Christ himself being the chief corner stone." The reference to the "apostles and prophets" points us to Holy Scripture. The ministry of the "apostles and prophets" was to bear witness to Christ, the "chief corner stone," and they did this by prophesying of his coming and writing about his gospel after his ascension. The Church is now built upon their testimony to him. This would not make much sense if we have lost access to their testimony. A foundation eaten by termites cannot support a house, and an absent foundation is even worse! Nevertheless, we have the promise from Christ that his Church will not be destroyed, "I say also unto thee, That thou art Peter, and upon this rock I will build my church; and the gates of hell shall not prevail against it" (Matthew 16:18). Given our immediate observation that the Church is still standing strong, we must conclude that God preserved his Word in a pure form in order to sustain the Church. We should also conclude that the Church will always have access to the text of Scripture.

Theological reflection also gives us a mechanism for how the work of preservation is carried out in history. Jesus prayed, "I have given unto them the words which thou gavest me" (John 17:8) and again in v. 20, "Neither pray I for these alone, but for them also which shall believe on me through their word." Christ delivered his words to the Apostles, and in faith they delivered them to the Church. This is the pattern that continues to this day. Christ has delivered his word to us through the past generations of believers, and we are to pass them on to the next generation. Paul affirms the same in 2 Timothy 2:2, "the things that thou hast heard of me among many witnesses, the same commit thou to faithful men, who shall be able to teach others also."

The doctrine of covenant is another way to understand this process of preservation. Covenant is the doctrine of God's gracious dealings with his people. It is a description of the promises he has made to men through Jesus Christ. Because of the sin of man, God's promises must not be conditioned upon our ability to perform any good. For instance, when the Bible promises forgiveness of sins, it does not condition that promise on our ability to do works of obedience. Likewise, when God promises to preserve his Word (which contains all his covenant promises), the fulfillment of that promise does not hinge on man's ability to do it. As we read in 1 Peter 1:24-25, "all flesh is as grass, and all the glory of man as the flower of grass. The grass withereth, and the flower thereof falleth away: But the word of the Lord endureth for ever." The promise of God to preserve the Bible is not conditioned on man's ability to accomplish the task. Just as one generation rises up and receives Scripture, that generation dies like grass. But the Lord is on his heavenly throne, and he will ensure that his Word to the Church is never lost.

Finally, it may help to look briefly at the historical witness, which the Church has made to the doctrine of preservation. When

I came to subscribe to the London Baptist Confession, I found it fit perfectly with what I already believed about the text of scripture. In fact, that was one of the reasons I looked further into confessional Christianity. In paragraph eight of chapter one of the confession, we read, "The Old Testament in Hebrew... and the New Testament in Greek... being immediately inspired by God, and by his singular care and providence kept pure in all ages, are therefore authentical." According to the confession, one of the conditions for the text of Scripture to be "authentical" is that it has been "kept pure in all ages." This is exactly what we have seen promised in the Scripture.

Practical: Using the Text

In April of 2016, I was ordained as a Pastor to serve at Open Door Baptist Church in Mayfield, Kentucky. I had just turned twenty-two at the time and with that calling came a weight of responsibility to shepherd the flock. There were occasions in which I felt over-whelmed, but I was enabled to make it through those times by applying the great doctrines of our faith to my ministry. One such doctrine was that of preservation, and I would like now to share how this doctrine practically applied in three particular areas (i.e., pastoral, evangelistic, and personal).

The central duty of a Pastor is to present the teachings of the Bible to the congregation and make application to their lives. One of the issues our church has worked through in recent years has been the proper form of corporate worship. I needed to address what kind of singing was permissible, or obligatory for us. I am convinced that proper worship must include the singing of Psalms, as Colossians 3:16 tells us, but this was a difficult issue to navigate because of unthinking allegiance to the way things have been done in the past. It caused me some anxiety. I can only imagine how much more difficult it would have been if I were unsure of what Scripture says about the topic, or if I had undermined our people's confidence in Scripture by questioning its text. Believing that God preserves his Word provides pastoral confidence. The people will notice and respect this.

I also had some struggles with whether I would leave a legacy. Many young ministers think they will have some wide recognition and impact, but when the humbling realities of local ministry set in, they are often discouraged from giving their best effort. Worse still, some will wonder, "What will happen to the congregation after I'm dead? Will it remain faithful?" This malaise can only be helped by resting in preservation. In Isaiah 55:11 God says, "So shall my word be that goeth forth out of my mouth: it shall not return unto me void, but it shall accomplish that which I please, and it shall prosper in the thing whereto I sent it." Note first the intention of God concerning his word: he himself secures its preservation. If God intends that Scripture speaks to his Church in every generation (Psalm 100:5), then he must preserve it to that end. That also means when a Pastor or teacher delivers the scriptural teaching faithfully, God will ensure that teaching has a lasting effect. It may not be seen in this lifetime, but it is sure to happen. Every faithful Pastor's ministry is made to prosper by the faithfulness of God.

Another practical application of preservation is confidence in evangelism. How are we to win the lost to Jesus Christ? Worldly tactics involve using entertainment or social activism to fill the church. Almost everyone has some kind of gimmick, but the Lord says in

Isaiah 40:6-8, "The voice said, Cry. And he said, What shall I cry? All flesh is grass, and all the goodliness thereof is as the flower of the field: The grass withereth, the flower fadeth: because the spirit of the LORD bloweth upon it: surely the people is grass. The grass withereth, the flower fadeth: but the word of our God shall stand for ever." If we build our evangelistic ministry on entertainment, we know that people will become disinterested. If we build it on current political ideas, we know that trends will change. But if we build it on the Word of our God, that is, the gospel, then we are offering something that will indeed stand forever. The preserved gospel is effectual (1 Thessalonians 2:13); it is relevant (1 Peter 1:23); it works particularly in particular lives (Hebrews 4:12), and it always will be as it is now.

One final point of personal application is that the preserved word of God confirms us in the gospel. We need regularly to be told "to him that worketh not, but believeth on him that justifieth the ungodly, his faith is counted for righteousness" (Romans 4:5). This is the ground for all the Christian life. If we cannot be sure that these are the pure words of God, then what can we do? If archaeologists found a copy of Romans without these words tomorrow, what personal hope could we have? What if some discovery of a text from an ancient Alexandrian sect was found, and it threw shades of doubt upon our understanding of terms like "faith" or "justification?" How would we know what to believe? If the reliability of holy Scripture is in question, we have no solid ground for our faith.

Tanner Dikin (Undergraduate studies, Boyce College) hosts the Sixth Church Podcast and is the Pastor of Open Door Baptist Church in Mayfield, Kentucky. He resides in Symsonia, Kentucky.

7

John Owen's Defense of the Received Text

William O. Einwechter

John Owen's treatise *Of the Integrity and Purity of the Hebrew and Greek Text of the Scripture* (*Collected Works*, Vol. 16, 345-421) offers a strong theological defense of the Received Text. The fact that his discourse is virtually unknown in our day, even amongst Reformed Christians, is an indicator of how the church has surrendered to the principles of modern textual criticism. To help remedy this shameful capitulation, this essay will provide a general overview of Owen's invaluable treatise.

The immediate occasion for Owen's treatise was the publication of the Polyglot Bible by Brian Walton. It printed the original Hebrew and Greek text along with various ancient versions and also included a massive appendix of variants. The broader historical context was Rome's attempt to discredit the Protestant doctrine of *sola scriptura* by pointing to textual variants as proof that the Greek New Testament was too corrupt to be considered authoritative. Their goal in this was to re-establish the authority of their church and the Latin Vulgate, thus derailing the Reformation. Owen's response to such attacks on *sola scriptura* remains highly relevant today.

Owen believed that the proper starting point for identifying the original text of Scripture was not to be found in "neutral" text critical principles determined by man's reason, but in the biblical doctrines of verbal inspiration and providential preservation. He lays the foundation for his defense of the purity of the Received Text by saying:

> The sum of what I am pleading for, as to the particular head to be vindicated, is, That as the Scriptures of the Old and New Testament were immediately and entirely given out by God himself, his mind being in them represented unto us without the least interveniency of such mediums and ways as were capable of giving change or alteration to the least iota or syllable; so, by his good and merciful providential dispensation, in his love to his word and church, his whole word, as first given out by him, is preserved unto us entire in the original languages; where, shining in its own beauty and lustre (as also in all translations, so far as they faithfully represent the originals), it manifests and evidences unto the consciences of men, without other foreign help or assistance, its divine original and authority (*Collected Works*, Vol. 16, 349-350; emphasis his).

Owen's claim is that we must presuppose inspiration and preservation if we are to interpret manuscript evidence aright. In other words, a theological *a priori* does have a place in the science of textual criticism! Having stated these theological presuppositions, he proceeds to explain the importance of them:

> Now, the several assertions or propositions contained in this position are to me such important truths, that I shall not be blamed in the least by my own spirit, nor I hope by any others, in contending for them, judging them fundamental parts of the faith once delivered to the saints; and though some of them may seem to be less weighty than others, yet they are so concatenated in themselves, that by the removal or destruction of any one of them, our interest in the others is utterly taken away. It will assuredly be granted that the persuasion of the coming forth of the word immediately from God, in the way pleaded for, is the foundation of all faith, hope, and obedience. But what, I pray, will it advantage us that God did so once deliver his word, if we are not assured also that that word so delivered hath been, by his special care and providence, preserved entire and uncorrupt unto us, or that it doth not evidence and manifest itself to be his word, being so preserved? Blessed, may we say, were the ages past, who received the word of God in its unquestionable power and purity, when it shone brightly in its own glorious native light, and was free from those defects and corruptions which, through the default of men in a long tract of time, it hath contracted; but for us, as we know not well where to lay

a sure foundation of believing that this book rather than any other doth contain what is left unto us of that word of his, so it is impossible we should ever come to any certainty almost of any individual word or expression whether it be from God or no. Far be it from the thoughts of any good man, that God, whose covenant with his church is that his word and Spirit shall never depart from it, Isa. lix. 21, Matt. v. 18, 1 Pet. i. 25, 1 Cor. xi. 23, Matt, xxviii. 20, hath left it in uncertainties about the things that are the foundation of all that faith and obedience which he requires at our hands (*Ibid.*, 350).

Having established this theological framework, Owen then expresses his horror that any *Christian* scholar would see the transmission of the biblical text as essentially the same as that of any other book. This is the prevailing view amongst today's critics and scholars, but for Owen, the doctrine of preservation calls for the recognition of the "extraordinary manner" in which the biblical text was transmitted. He contends that the transcribers of the original copies, guided by the faith of the church, possessing a clear sense of the importance of their work, and by the superintending providence of God, exercised a "religious care and diligence" in their work. Therefore, to view the process of copying Scripture as no different than transcribing the old heathen authors (e.g., Homer, Aristotle, Tully) is "not tolerable in a Christian" and a virtual denial of the care of God for his Word and for his church (*Ibid.*, 355-356).

Owen then draws his discussion to a close by emphatically rejecting the view that the question of the transmission of Scripture is strictly a matter of historical investigation:

It can, then, with no colour of probability be asserted (which yet I find some learned men too free in granting), namely, that there hath the same fate attended the Scripture in its transcription as hath done other books. Let me say without offence, this imagination, asserted on deliberation, seems to me to border on atheism. Surely the promise of God for the preservation of his word, with his love and care of his church, of whose faith and obedience that word of his is the only rule, requires other thoughts at our hands (*Ibid.*, 357).

Owen finally establishes twelve propositions that elucidate how Scripture was kept pure in all ages:

1. The *providence of God* in taking care of his word, which he hath magnified above all his name, as the most glorious product of his wisdom and goodness, his great concernment in this word answering his promise to this purpose;

2. The *religious care* of the church (I speak not of the Romish synagogue) to whom these oracles of God were committed;

3. The care of the first writers in giving out *authentic copies* of what they had received from God unto many, which might be rules to the first transcribers;

4. The *multiplying copies* to such a number that it was impossible any should corrupt them all, wilfully or by negligence;

5. The preservation of *authentic copies*, first in the Jewish synagogues, then in the Christian assemblies, with reverence and diligence;

6. The *daily reading* and studying of the word by all sorts of persons, ever since its first writing, rendering every alteration liable to immediate observation and discovery, and that all over the world; with,

7. The consideration of the many *millions* that looked on every letter and tittle in this book as their inheritance, which for the whole world they would not be deprived of: and in particular, for the Old Testament (now most questioned [i.e., in Owen's day]);

8. The care of Ezra and his companions, *the men of the great synagogue*, in restoring the Scripture to its purity when it had met with the greatest trial that it ever underwent in this world, considering the paucity of the copies then extant;

9. The *care of the Masoretes* from his days and downward, to keep perfect and give an account of every syllable in the Scripture...;

10. The *constant consent* of all copies in the world, so that, as sundry learned men have observed, there is not in the whole Mishna, Gemara, or either Talmud, any one place of Scrip-

ture found otherwise read than as it is now in our copies;

11. The security we have that no mistakes were voluntarily or negligently brought into the text before the coming of our Saviour, who was to *declare* all things, in that he not once reproves the Jews on that account, when yet for their false glosses on the word he spares them not;

12. Afterward the watchfulness which the two nations of Jews and Christians had always one upon the other,—with sundry things of the like importance, might to this purpose be insisted on (*Ibid.*, 358).

God's wonderful workings through divine providence in the preservation of his Word, led Owen to affirm with great certainty "the purity of the present original copies of the Scripture, or rather copies in the original languages, which the church of God doth now and hath for many ages enjoyed as her chiefest treasure" (*Ibid.*, 353). He confidently asserted "that *the whole Scripture*, entire as given out from God, without any loss, is preserved in the *copies of the originals* yet remaining.... In them all, we say, is every letter and tittle of the word" (*Ibid.*, 357). Because of "the providential preservation of the whole book of God... we may have full assurance that we enjoy the whole revelation of his will in the copies abiding amongst us...." (*Ibid.*, 367). Surely, "every letter and tittle of the word of God remains in the copies preserved by his merciful providence for the use of his church" (*Ibid.*, 359).

The preserved "copies of the originals" of which Owen wrote

was the Received Text, and he therefore rejected the idea that it should be amended by human conjecture, by readings in obviously corrupt codices, by readings that differ from "the concurrent consent of all others that are extant in the world," or by translations of the biblical text (*Ibid.*, 366). For Owen, the common received text of Scripture was the sole standard for judging doctrine, translations, or textual variants. Owen states:

> Let it be remembered that the vulgar copy we use was the public possession of many generations,—that upon the invention of prin-ting it was in actual authority throughout the world with them that used and understood that language... let that, then, pass for the standard, which is confessedly its right and due.... (*Ibid.*, 366).

Theodore Letis summarizes: "Owen was calling for a *canonical* view of the text, or the text as canon, by which to assess variants—but variants from the providentially preserved, canonical form of the texts of Scripture" (Theodore Letis, "John Owen Versus Brian Walton: A Reformed Response to the Birth of Text Criticism," in *The Majority Text: Essays and Reviews in the Continuing Debate*, 161).

Owen, as a Calvinist, knew "the vanity, curiosity, pride, and naughtiness of the heart of man" (*Collected Works*, Vol. 16, 363) and thus recognized that the boldness of the critics in attacking the Received Text was not due primarily to a desire to give the church a better text, but rather to collect and publish variants as evidence of their own scholarship. More significantly, Owen saw their rejection of the doctrine of preservation as theologically motivated, and predicted that it would be used as a principal tool of Satan:

> What use hath been made, and is as yet made, in the world, of
> this supposition, that corruptions have befallen the originals
> of the Scripture, which those various lections at first view
> seem to intimate, I need not declare. It is, in brief, the foun-
> dation of Mohammedanism (Alcor. Azoar. 5), the chiefest
> and principal prop of Popery, the only pretense of fanatical
> anti-scripturalists, and the root of much hidden atheism in
> the world.... How far... [men] may be strengthened in their
> infidelity by the consideration of these things [i.e., the sup-
> posed corruption of the originals] time will manifest (*Ibid.*,
> 348).

Surely, says Owen, the assumption that the Received Text is corrupt would become

> ...as an engine suited to the destruction of the important truth
> before pleaded for [i.e., verbal inspiration and providential
> preservation], and as a fit weapon put into the hands of men
> of atheistical minds and principles, such as this age abounds
> withal, to oppose the whole evidence of truth revealed in the
> Scripture. I fear, with some, either the pretended infallible
> judge [the Roman Church] or the depth of atheism will be
> found to lie at the door of these considerations (*Ibid.*, 352-353).

Owen, unlike his Reformed descendants of today, was keenly aware of the theological issues that were at stake in the textual debates of his day. He had witnessed firsthand how "The papists have ploughed with their heifer to disparage the original, and to cry up the Vulgar Latin" (*Ibid.*, 362). He also saw how naturalistic text-critical principles set aside preservation, undermined scriptural authority, and worked "to frighten poor unstable souls into the arms of the pretended infallible guide" (*Ibid.*, 365). Owen solemnly warned the Protestant Church: "We went from Rome under the conduct *of the purity* of the originals; I wish none have a mind to return thither again under the pretense of their *corruption*" (Ibid., 370).

Textual criticism has never been, and never will be, a neutral enterprise carried out by scholars who just want to know the "facts." Every textual critic approaches his work with definite presuppositions concerning the nature of Scripture and the locus of authority for determining the true text. Owen's work helps us to understand that there are really only three approaches to textual criticism: (1) the Protestant approach which presupposes the authority of Scripture to delimit the true text by means of divine inspiration and preservation; (2) the Roman Catholic approach which presupposes the authority of the Papacy to define the text of Scripture by means of the pronouncement of the Pope or Councils; and (3) the "anti-scripturalist" (or "atheist") approach which presupposes the authority of man's reason to determine the text according to the scientific method.

In our day, the third method reigns supreme among both liberal and evangelical scholars (though the latter would be indignant at having their "scholarly" method labeled as "anti-scripturalist" or "atheist"). Nevertheless, it is undeniable that their methodology is naturalistic to the core. It arose during the era of the Enlightenment when men cast off the authority of divine revelation and replaced it with the authority of human reason; advocating for full human autonomy and the power of man's intellect to establish truth and morality.

Biblical scholars then applied this new perspective to textual criticism and ended up treating the Bible as any other book, establishing naturalistic canons of criticism to use in determining the "true text." These scholars were adamant in their belief that the Received Text was corrupt and were united in their goal to "dethrone" the canonical text and replace it with one of their own making. The results can be seen today in the Nestle-Aland (NA) and United Bible Societies (UBS) editions of the Greek New Testament. It is upon these editions that most modern translations are based.

Owen's treatise, however, exposes modern Enlightenment textual criticism for what it truly is and calls us to return to the classical approach to textual criticism and to the canonical texts of the Reformation. Let us, therefore, embrace the theological foundations of verbal inspiration and providential preservation, and cast off the humanistic theories and methods of modern textual criticism. Once we are freed from the grip of naturalistic thinking, the church will once again be able to confess its faith in the purity of Scripture and enjoy a great measure of certainty (instead of the current "cannot know for sure" view of the text).

Recovering the confessional Reformed view of God's providential preservation of Scripture, as taught by Owen, is necessary for fulfilling the Great Commission of discipling the nations, as it is only upon the sure foundation of faith in the purity of Scripture that this great work can be done.

William O. Einwechter (B.A. Washington Bible College; Th.M. Capital Bible Seminary) is a teaching elder at Immanuel Free Reformed Church in Stevens,

Pennsylvania. He is the author of "English Bible Translations: By What Standard?" He and his wife Linda are the parents of ten children.

8

Preaching in the Name of the Amen

Brent C. Evans

"And unto the angel of the church of the Laodiceans write; These things saith the Amen, the faithful and true witness, the beginning of the creation of God" (Revelation 3:14). The Laodicean "angel" had a work of difficulty before him, and it was like the work that we ministers of the Word have before us today in these times of luke-warm Christianity. First of all, we have personal heart-work to do: "Be zealous therefore, and repent" (v. 19). Next, we have work to do in preaching as Christ's "angels" or messengers. Both our personal heart-work and our public preaching-work begin with receiving the written Word from Christ: "unto the angel of the church of the Laodiceans write..." (v. 14).

While there are many reasons for doing so, this article contains one element of my testimony as to why I preach from the Scriptures that have been received from Christ by his ministers and church since the beginning (cf. Deuteronomy 31:9, 26; Romans 3:2), and therefore why I do not follow the ever-emerging and always-uncertain text promulgated more recently by the post-Enlightenment academy, where God is not feared. After twelve years in the gospel ministry, I have become settled in the conviction that the use of the Received Text of Scripture is an important starting point for what we may call, in reference to Revelation 3:14, *preaching in the name of the Amen.*

As preachers, we should constantly stir ourselves up to consider *whose* word it is that we are handling. Christ's glory as the great prophet of his church shines forth through the name that he gives unto himself: "the Amen, the faithful and true witness." "'Amen' is a short word," said Richard Sibbes, "but marvellously pregnant, full of sense, full of spirit." He suggests three meanings of this little word: "'Amen:' it is so. Nay, 'Amen:' it shall be so. Nay, 'Amen:' be it so, or let it be so" (*Works*, Vol. 6, 540). God uses this word to seal his own truthfulness, and we use it to signify our assent to his truth, our hearty trust in him as the God of truth, and our desire for the fulfillment of his Word. There are four ways that Christ is the Amen unto his church through his Spirit and his Word written and preached.

Christ is the Amen *essentially*. Christ does not simply say "Amen," but he is the Amen. He is the very "God of truth," or "God of Amen," as the word runs (Isaiah 65:16). In his eternity he is unchangingly faithful. In his righteousness he cannot lie. In his wisdom he cannot be baffled or uncertain. In his power he cannot be beaten back from fulfilling his Word. In his goodness he would not be so cruel as to speak falsely.

Christ is the Amen *extensively*. He is the Amen of the whole Bible, sealing the whole counsel of God. He affirms the whole Old Testament with a "verily," or "Amen" (Matthew 5:17-18). When he expounds the spirituality of the law, he adds his "verily," or "Amen" (Matthew 5:26). Indeed, the very presence of the Hebrew word "Amen" in the Greek New Testament indicates that in the gospel of our Lord Jesus Christ we preach him as the fulfillment of all the types and prophecies of the Old Testament, now held forth unto all nations to be believed upon.

Christ is the Amen *evangelically*. While Christ upholds all the commandments and threatenings contained in the Bible, he is especially the Amen of the promises. "For all the promises of God in him are yea, and in him Amen, unto the glory of God by us" (2 Corinthians 1:20). The gospel is "a new volume of truths which had not been true, if he by his blood had not made them so" (Thomas Goodwin, *Christ Our Mediator*, 102).

Christ is the Amen *experimentally*. Christ alone opens the understanding and the heart to receive his truth. He anoints the eyes of the blind that they may see. "There is such an inward rising of the heart, and an innate rebellion against the blessed truth of God," said Richard Sibbes, "that unless God, by his strong arm, bring the heart down, it never will nor can say, 'Amen'" (*Works*, Vol. 6, 540).

This should quicken within us a hearty desire habitually to live and labor in the sight of Christ the Amen! Every time we come to the word "Amen" in the scriptures, there is an evident opportunity to lift up our hearts unto Christ the Amen and enjoy fellowship with him in the glory of that faithfulness and truth that pervades his whole Word. Our God is a faithful promiser, and therefore the faith must be professed without wavering, beginning with us who preach (Hebrews 10:23).

The modern critical text omits the word "Amen" in many places in the New Testament where the Received Text retains it. Perhaps the most obvious instance of this is that the critical text omits "Amen" by omitting the conclusion of the Lord's Prayer (Matthew 6:13). Furthermore, the "Amen" is omitted from the end of each of the four Gospels, and from the end of 1-2 Corinthians, Ephesians, Philippians, Colossians, 1-2 Thessalonians, 1-2 Timothy, Titus, Philemon, Hebrews, 1-2 Peter, 1-2 John, and Revelation. Though the "Amen" seems to have fared better in the critical text in places where it comes in the midst of a New Testament book, it is also sometimes omitted in these cases, as for example at Romans 16:20. What has been said above should make it clear that this is a matter of weight and importance. The omission of any instance of the word "Amen" would not merely be a matter of style or ritualistic formality, but a matter of the glory of Christ, the Amen. Upon reflection, both in study and preaching, the word "Amen" in the Received Text proves suitable to its context and precious to the hearts of sincere hearers.

The word "Amen" carries in its own bosom a strong argument for using the text of Scripture that has been received and used down through the centuries, and not a recently-promoted, provisionally-reconstructed text. Moses commanded the people, when they confirmed the covenant on Ebal and Gerizim, to say "Amen" (Deuteronomy 27:15 ff.). When the time came to carry this out, Joshua took the book of the law that Moses had written and entrusted to the Levites (Deuteronomy 31:9), and "read all the words of the law, the blessings and cursings, according to all that is written in the

book of the law. There was not a word of all that Moses commanded, which Joshua read not before all the congregation of Israel..."
(Joshua 8:34-35). The people could say "Amen" because the book of
the law had been preserved. They could avouch the Lord to be their
God in accordance with the terms of the covenant that he had not
only fixed, but transmitted to them uncorrupted in the scriptures
that had been providentially preserved and received in the Old
Testament church.

On God's side, the "Amen" says that he has settled the terms
of the covenant of grace that he is offering to us. On our side, the
"Amen" says that we receive his offer and its terms as authentic, that
we believe God, and that we take him to be our God. If the book
of the law had been lost, or altered, or if there had been a need
for an ongoing process of recovering the words that Moses wrote,
the people of Joshua's day should have withheld their "Amen" until
they got clarity about what God's Word to them was. By this logic,
the modern (or post-modern) textual critics should remove every
instance of "Amen" from the Bible, since their text is in constant
flux. Indeed, if the "Amen" is removed, the sinner standing upon
Ebal will remain unconvinced in his conscience that he deserves
the curse of the law, and therefore will feel no need for the altar that
Joshua erected upon Ebal (Joshua 8:30). When the "Amen" goes out
of the Bible, the curse of the law and the blessing of the gospel go
out too.

What has been said to defend the omissions of "Amen" from
the modern critical text? While a thorough survey is beyond the
scope of this article, it may be helpful to note a statement by Paul D.
Wegner in *A Student's Guide to Textual Criticism of the Bible: Its His-*

tory, Methods & Results, in which he refers to a particular example. In his section on "intentional changes" to the text, under a subsection on "additions and glosses," Wegner makes the following comment about the "Amen" at the end of Luke's Gospel: "Some manuscripts of Luke 24:53 add the word ἀμήν ('amen') at the end of the verse which suggests that some thought a Gospel should end this way (see mss of Matthew 28:20; A², Δ, Θ, etc.)" (54).

Wegner says that "some manuscripts" of Luke 24:53 "add the word ἀμήν." At the time of this writing, the Institute for New Testament Text Research has cataloged 1,045 Greek manuscripts that contain Luke 24:53 (ntvmr.uni-muenster.de/liste. Accessed May 31, 2021). Meanwhile, the current edition of the critical text appears to list only 14 Greek manuscripts (omitting lectionaries, versions, and patristic evidence) that end Luke's Gospel with the word "God" and omit the "Amen." Thus, rather than saying that "some manuscripts" add an "Amen," it would be more accurate to say that roughly 99% of the extant Greek manuscripts are witnesses to the authenticity of Luke's final "Amen." This majority of witnesses indicates that across the centuries, Christ's church has received and used a version of Luke's Gospel that ends with "Amen." Luke ends with "Amen" in *Codex Alexandrinus* (fifth century), multiple uncial manuscripts from the ninth century, and numerous minuscule manuscripts, including the Byzantine text tradition. Extant evidence suggests that when Tatian wrote his Diatessaron in the mid-second century, the copy of Luke's Gospel available to him ended with "Amen." Even Westcott and Hort's "neutral" text, the fourth-century *Codex Vaticanus*, ends Luke with an "Amen."

Because "some manuscripts" have an "Amen" at Luke 24:53, Wegner says that this suggests "that some thought a Gospel should end this way." The statement comes in Wegner's section on "intentional changes," and he appears to be offering an analysis of the intentions of the copyists who altered the scriptures at this point. This statement is open to objection. To remove the ecclesiastically-received "Amen" at Luke 24:53 on the basis of a minority of witnesses is one thing, but to speculate about the inward thinking of the copyists who supposedly added a word to Scripture intentionally is a further step. The manuscripts bear witness to what they wrote, but not to what they were thinking. To suggest, without evidence, that some scribes elevated stylistic coherence above fidelity to the Word of God is, at least, careless, and, at worst, may amount to slander. It is the written Word of God that is able to search our hearts (Hebrews 4:12), not we who are able to search the hearts of those who copied it.

The absence of Luke's final "Amen" in early manuscripts like P75 and *Codex Sinaiticus*, both of which were brought forth out of obscurity in recent history, is not sufficient reason to overturn the text that God providentially preserved in his church in all ages, and that his church has received because it is the Word of God (cf. WCF, 1.4 and 1.8). At present, we may not have sufficient light to explain fully why there is variation in the manuscript evidence, but we do have sufficient light to recognize and receive the final "Amen" in Luke, and the other "Amens" in the Received Text of Scripture, as the Word of God.

It is fitting that Luke ended his Gospel with an "Amen" after beginning on the note of certainty: "That thou mightest know the *certainty* of those things, wherein thou hast been instructed" (Luke 1:4, emphasis added). Matthew Henry appears to have thought that the hearers might even join in with their "Amen" at the conclusion of the reading of this gospel:

> The *amen* that concludes seems to be added by the church and every believer to the reading of the gospel, signifying an assent to the truths of the gospel, and a hearty concurrence with all the disciples of Christ in praising and blessing God. *Amen*. Let him be continually praised and blessed.

While Henry suggests that the "Amen" was "added" by the church, it seems that he meant something different from what Metzger meant when, in his *Textual Commentary*, he called this "Amen" a "liturgical addition introduced by copyists" (191). Metzger was speaking of an alteration of Luke's Gospel. Henry was speaking of a sum-total effect or fruit of Luke's gospel, the "Amen" of faith, lifted up by and with the final "Amen" in the text itself. What wisdom on the part of God the Holy Ghost that he inspired the concluding word "Amen" so that it might be there in the text and then taken up on the lips of those in whose hearts he would work faith through the Word!

Brethren, let us preach confidently from the Scriptures we have received from the Amen who has written to the "angels" of his churches. While textual critics go on speculating about what the Bible may once have said, we preachers should go on offering Christ's sealed testament to perishing sinners, entreating men to set their "Amen" to it. In our congregation, when we have partaken of the testament-sealing sacrament of the Lord's Supper, we conclude by singing from the metrical translation of Psalm 72. How glorious it is to lift up our hearts and voices to heaven when we sing the double "Amen" at the end!

"His name forever shall endure; last like the sun it shall:
Men shall be blessed in him, and bless'd all nations shall him call.
Now blessed be the Lord our God, the God of Israel,
For he alone doth wondrous works, in glory that excel.
And blessed be his glorious name to all eternity:
The whole earth let his glory fill. Amen, so let it be."

Brent C. Evans (B.S. University of Connecticut; M.Div. Reformed Theological Seminary) is the Pastor of Reformation Presbyterian Church, Free Church of Scotland (Continuing) in Snellville, Georgia, and resides in the area with his wife and three children.

9

Should We Use Those Proof Texts?

Philip Gardiner

John Owen said that a Pastor's "first and principal duty... is to feed the flock by diligent preaching of the word" (*Collected Works*, Vol. 16, 74). In order that the Pastor may effectively teach and apply the Word of God, he must first be convinced of its truthfulness and reliability. It is no surprise that Owen, having declared the duty of the Minister, was also able to speak of the reliability of the scriptures. He spoke of God's "good and merciful providential dispensation" through which "his whole word, as given out by him is preserved unto us entire in the original languages" (*Collected Works*, Vol. 16, 350). Owen was affirming God's preservation of the Word down through the ages, so that a faithful text would always be available for the saints of God. The logical outworking of Owen's argument is that the Preacher who lacks certainty in the content of Scripture will lack confidence in teaching and applying it to the flock. As the Pastor comes to portions of Scripture that are disputed, he will have no confidence in declaring what God has said.

I am very thankful to the Lord that I was introduced to the Authorized Version (AV) of scripture in my childhood. The congregation in which I was raised did not take a strict Received Text position and so during my teenage years I was introduced to other versions. I now smile in reflection, but during those years I thought that those who used the New International Version (NIV) were serious about actually trying to understand the Bible, while those who continued to use the AV were not! I was delighted when I received my first copy of the NIV, but was soon disappointed when reading the book of Job. Simply having a modern translation did not make that book any easier to understand!

I now realize that I had fallen into the same trap that many of today's Christians have fallen into: presuming that the rise of the modern versions was simply the outworking of making the English Bible easier to understand. I had not yet wrestled through a more foundational question; namely, that the different English versions are actually based on different Greek texts: the Received Text and the modern Critical Text. The differences between these text platforms must be considered.

During my upbringing, I was completely unaware that there were passages, verses, and words that were disputed in the New Testament. Given my ignorance on this matter, I was rather perplexed when I saw a sign-board at the church I later began to attend. It stated that only the Authorized Version was used. I wondered why a church would take that position, when the modern versions should be easier for a modern audience to understand. When 1 met with the Minister, Rev. Ron Johnstone, 1 asked him why that was the case. The Pastor's wise answers emphasized the underlying textual issues, a matter that 1 had not previously considered. Secondary arguments for retaining the AV or emotional arguments of attachment to the version were not raised in that conversation. 1 was blessed in that first conversation to be brought to the heart of the issue, the underlying Greek text.

After my call to the ministry 1 was blessed to be able to study in a Bible College that upholds the Received Text position and thereafter to minister within a denomination that does the same. In 2014, 1 moved from Northern Ireland to Australia to take up the Pastorate of Perth Free Presbyterian Church, one of a small group of Australian churches under the care of the Free Presbyterian Church of Ulster. During my time here, 1 have occasionally had the opportunity to minister to children and adults who do not have English as their first language. While using the AV in such circumstances has sometimes been a challenge, it has also provided me an opportunity to test my conviction regarding the textual matter. 1 am appreciative of those editions of the Authorized Version that seek to help with the antiquated words by giving helpful substitutes in the margin.

1 count it a privilege to minister in a confessional church and have been appreciative of the usage of the term "the confessional text." In considering the confession and catechisms of the Westminster divines, my attention has been drawn in recent years to some of their proof texts. The divines were aware of the danger of proof texting, namely "a text without a context is a pretext for a proof text." The divines did not see proof texts as the sole basis for

reaching their theological conclusions, but held to the analogy of scripture which interprets individual passages in light of the whole testimony of Scripture. The proof texts then are merely providing a starting place, yet in many cases an important starting place for exploring the various doctrines in the confession. The divines would have exhorted that proof texts be considered in their context.

What strikes me as significant is that some of the proof texts for vital doctrines in the confession are the very texts that are questioned by the modern Critical Text. For example, in chapter 2, dealing with the orthodox doctrine of the Trinity, the divines state, "In the unity of the Godhead there be three Persons of one substance, power, and eternity: God the Father, God the Son, and God the Holy Ghost." One of the proof texts for this statement is what scholars refer to as the *Comma Johanneum* or Johannine Comma, "For there are three that bear record in heaven, the Father, the Word, and the Holy Ghost" (1 John 5:7). Though the *Comma Johanneum* is one of the more difficult passages in the textual debate, it is significant that the writers of the confession demonstrated confidence in its authenticity.

In chapter 8, dealing with Christ the Mediator, the divines discussed Christ's person as God and man: "...two whole, perfect, and distinct natures, the Godhead and the manhood, were inseparably joined together in one person, without conversion, composition, or confusion." One of the proof texts is the great statement of 1 Timothy 3:16, "God was manifest in the flesh." Some anti-trinitarian writers have argued that the critical text supports their theory that Christ was not God, following the translation "he appeared in a body." Dr. Alan Cairns states, "it is true that there is plenty of other proof of the doctrine [of Christ's deity], but that is no reason to be complacent about throwing away one of the greatest and clearest statements on the subject" (*Dictionary of Theological Terms*, 3rd edition, 471).

Another significant example of the divines' adherence to the Received Text is Question and Answer 107 of the *Shorter Catechism*, "What doth the conclusion of the Lord's prayer teach us?" The conclusion referred to is "For thine is the kingdom, and the power, and the glory, for ever, Amen" (Matthew 6:13b). Children who are raised using modern versions based on the Critical Text may struggle to find this doxology in their Bibles! The divines, however, had no doubts regarding its authenticity. It must seem a strange thing for families who make use of some of the modern versions which omit this clause to defend the inclusion of this question in the Catechism.

What is true of the work of the Westminster divines is also true of the writers of the Heidelberg Catechism. The first proof text of the Lord's ascension in Question and Answer 46 is taken from the so-called longer ending of Mark's Gospel (Mark 16:19). Mark 16:16 is also included in Question and Answer 69 dealing with baptism as a sign and seal. Clearly, the writers of the Catechism would not have agreed with today's scholars that the traditional ending of Mark's Gospel is spurious or strange.

While the Authorized Version states in Revelation 1:5 that Christ's blood has "washed us," most of the modern versions adopt the critical text reading of "freed us" or "loosed us." Interestingly, the Heidelberg Catechism supports the Received Text reading, presenting it as part of its proof that the believer is washed in Christ's blood (Question and Answer 70).

It strikes me as unusual to think that one might subscribe to the historic Reformed Confessions and Catechisms while arguing that the divines were mistaken in the proof texts, because they were working from corrupted manuscripts. Such a view makes the framers of the Confessions and Catechisms appear to be confused when they speak of God's "singular care and providence" of his Word. The divines spoke of the "purity" of God's Word in all ages, claiming that these scriptures are therefore "authentical" (WCF, 1.8). Is it not inconsistent to claim agreement with the divines on that point, and yet charge them with making use of inauthentic scriptures?

The chief desire of the Preacher is to be biblical. There are godly men who have embraced the modern Critical Text who solidly declare the doctrine of the Trinity, who uphold the deity of Christ, and strongly believe in praising God in prayer, "ascribing kingdom, power, and glory to him" (WSC, 107). It is true that their rejection of the Received Text has not caused them to deny the truth of orthodox doctrine or the reality of Christian living. The one doctrine however, that has been affected by the views of the Critical Text is the doctrine of Scripture. While holding to inspiration, they may have certain questions about preservation. However, those two doctrines stand together. If God has not providentially preserved his Word, how can we be sure *what* he inspired?

I rejoice in the blessing in being able to stand before a congregation and say, "[God's] word is truth" (John 17:17). What a blessing for the congregation to reply in worship to the Almighty God, "Thy word *is* true *from* the beginning" (Psalm 119:160).

Philip Gardiner (B.Sc. University of Ulster; Dipl. Whitefield College of the Bible, Northern Ireland) is Pastor of Perth Free Presbyterian Church in Western Australia, where he lives with his wife and their two daughters.

10

The Reformed Christian's Text

Dane Johannsson

There are many good reasons for retaining the received, or traditional, text of the Bible in our reading, preaching, and teaching. The book of essays you now hold in your hands bears witness to this fact. In addition to the authors of these essays, a multitude of men have given extensive reasons and defenses for using the Received Text. Dr. Joel Beeke, in his online article, *"Thirteen Practical Reasons for Retaining the King James Version of the Bible,"* gives, in my opinion, some of the best. For over a century, the Trinitarian Bible Society has published hundreds of sermons, lectures, articles, and tracts in support of retaining the Received Text. To all these reasons, I give hearty approval.

In this article, I will focus on just one of the reasons I read, preach, and teach from the Received Text, namely, that it is the Reformed

Christian's text. Discussions among Reformed brethren concerning the text of Scripture are often bogged down with lengthy diatribes upon textual variation, the "which TR" argument, or other, albeit important, but nonetheless, tertiary issues. One of the main points for Reformed Christians to consider in the study of textual criticism is this: irrefutably, the men who produced the Reformed confessions used and defended the Received Text.

I am honored to serve in a local congregation that upholds the Reformed confessions of faith. As a member in this congregation, I take these confessions seriously. They serve as cherished guides for my faith, practice, and ministry. I regularly use the Westminster Standards, 1689 London Baptist Confession, and the Belgic Confession in my ministry. In my previous ministry experience, it was my practice each Lord's Day to read and briefly expound a portion from one of the confessions, as well as preach through the Heidelberg Catechism yearly in our mid-week service. I take a catholic (i.e., universal) approach to the Reformed faith. The confessions supplement one another, and although they differ in specific emphases and articulation, they teach one and the same biblical and Reformed faith. Therefore, what the confessions teach regarding the main *loci* of theology ought to be taken seriously by Reformed Christians, especially ministers. This includes Bibliology.

If I believe the doctrines that these men have put forward in the confessions, then I have to consider what text they formulated these doctrines by, and I must also take seriously what they believed and taught *about* that text. What text did these men have, and what did they believe about it? What was their doctrine of Holy Scripture, specifically in relation to the text then in their hands? The text which they had and used was the Received Text, and they believed that this text was inspired, infallible, and preserved. A person cannot, with any honesty, deny that the text of the Magisterial Reformers and the post-reformation divines was the received, or traditional text. This *is* the text of the Reformed tradition, and that tradition has universally taught that this is the providentially preserved text, originally inspired by the Holy Spirit, and thus, infallible.

The Reformed Doctrine of Holy Scripture

Looking to the English branch of the Reformed church, it is evident that the men of the English Reformation believed that the text of Scripture had been providentially preserved. They confessed that the text in their hands was the text that God had both inspired and preserved. The Westminster Confession (1646), the Savoy Declaration (1658), and the London Baptist Confession of Faith (1689) all state, in chapter one, paragraph eight, that the original Hebrew and Greek texts of Scripture were "immediately inspired by God" and have been "by his singular care and providence kept pure in all ages." They believed that the text in their hands was "therefore authentical" and so much so, that "in all controversies of religion the church is finally to appeal unto them." Thus, believing Paul's words, that "All scripture is given by inspiration of God, and is profitable for doctrine" (2 Timothy 3:16) and receiving the text then in their hands as the preserved form of the inspired original, they we not ashamed to defend doctrines from such passages as Matthew 6:13b, Mark 16:9-20, John 1:18, 1 Timothy 3:16, 1 John 5:7, among other traditional readings now disputed by modern textual critics. While it is easily demonstrated that they *used* the Received Text, we must also ask what they believed *about* the Received Text, theologically.

The Irish theologian, James Ussher, whose classic work, *A Body of Divinity* was so influential upon those who framed the Westminster Standards, wrote that the "marvelous preservation of the Scriptures" demonstrated their divine inspiration, and that God had by his providential care "preserved them, and every part of them" (*A Body of Divinity*, 8). For Ussher, no part of Scripture had ever fallen away or been corrupted.

David Dickson, one of the Scottish commissioners to the Westminster Assembly, as well as the Confession's earliest and most reliable interpreter, wrote that since God had, by his singular care and providence, kept the text of Scripture pure in all ages, we can thus conclude that the Papists grievously erred by maintaining that the "fountains," that is, the original Hebrew and Greek texts of the Bible, were corrupted. He supported his claim that the scriptures have been providentially preserved without corruption by pointing to Christ's words in Matthew 5:18, where Jesus says that not "one jot or one tittle" shall pass away from God's Word. Furthermore, Dickson argued that it is not possible to prove that the text of Scripture has been corrupted, and even if someone said that they *could* prove it, we should not believe them, because, "if any such corruption had been in the Scripture, Christ and his apostles" would have "declared so much" (*Truth's Victory Over Error*, 12). In other words, Dickson's argument is that if the Bible was corrupted in any place, the Bible itself would have plainly told us this, which it does not.

Thomas Watson was another able interpreter of the Westminster Standards, and in his commentary on the Shorter Catechism, he stated:

We may know the Scripture to be the Word of God by its miraculous preservation in all ages.... Nor has the church of God, in all revolutions and changes, kept the Scripture that it should not be lost only, but that it should not be depraved. The *letter* of Scripture has been preserved, without any corruption, in the original tongue (*A Body of Divinity*, 19).

John Owen, often called the "prince of the puritans" and one of the chief framers of the Savoy Declaration (a Congregationalist revision of the WCF), wrote, "the Scriptures of the Old and New Testament [which] were immediately and entirely given out by God himself... [are] by his good and merciful providential dispensation... preserved unto us entire in the original languages" (*Collected Works,* Vol. 16, 351-352).

The men who penned the English Reformed confessions, and their later interpreters, believed the inspired text of Scripture had been perfectly and providentially preserved by God, down to the very letter, and that this text was then in their hands. All Reformed ministers must seriously consider what these great men of the past believed on this point and how it relates to the theology of modern textual criticism. It cannot be denied that the theology of Scripture articulated by these past luminaries is quite different than that put forward by contemporary evangelicals, even those who are professedly-reformed, but who still hold to modern textual criticism. This is demonstrated by comparing the Reformed view with this quote from Dan Wallace, representative of the view of modern evangelical textual criticism:

We do not have now—in our critical Greek texts or any translations thereof—exactly what the authors of the New Testament wrote. Even if we did, we would not know it. There are many, many places in which the text of the New Testament is uncertain (Hixson and Gurry, eds., *Myths and Mistakes in New Testament Textual Criticism*, xii).

One of these things is not like the other, and one of these things is not an orthodox view of Scripture. My conscience is bound to the scriptures, and my doctrinal heritage has accurately articulated what the Bible says about itself. Therefore, I both reject the theology of modern textual criticism and hold to the Received Text.

The Received Text: The Reformed Pastor's Text

Holding a confessional view of the text is only the beginning, since the confessions themselves call for vulgar transitions of it. The most widely accepted, received, and utilized English translation of the Received Text is the Authorized (or King James) Version of the Bible. We can confidently say that no document in the history of the world has been more commented upon, picked through, preached, examined, or critiqued than the Received Text of the Bible *via* the Authorized Version (AV). Scads of commentaries upon portions of, or the whole of it, are still in print. The best of these come from the Reformed tradition. The Westminster "proofs from scripture" use the AV as their text. Matthew Henry based his magisterial six volume commentary of the whole Bible upon it. The eighteenth century Particular Baptist, John Gill, also used it in his nine volume commentary. The Scottish commentators all used it, as well as the best of the nineteenth century Southern Presbyterians. In short, for over four centuries, the Received Text, *via* translation in the Authorized Version, has been the touchstone and standard of all Reformed Bible preaching and commentary.

In my ministry, I have no greater ally than the AV. It is the *text* of English Reformed theology. In my preparations to teach the Bible, I have an arsenal of solid, orthodox, Reformed interpretation at my fingertips. When preparing a sermon, I know that I can turn to Matthew Poole, Matthew Henry, David Dickson, James Durham, John Gill, Thomas Goodwin, Thomas Manton, Joseph Caryl, William Jenkyn, William Gouge, and find the most helpful, experiential, practical, and trustworthy comments available in the English language. All of them are based upon the same exact text and translation. The works of these men minister to me daily in my personal devotions and study. Here I have a blessed and happy continuity in my life and ministry. When my fire is burning low I can open the sermons of Thomas Brooks, William Gurnall, Charles Spurgeon, John Flavel, and Martyn Lloyd-Jones, confident that I will find hot coals upon their hearths. All these men preached eminently useful sermons from the Authorized Version. It is heartening to use the same text and translation utilized by the best English commentators and preachers of the past.

The Received Text in the Reformed Pew

I believe the Received Text is most beneficial to those in the pew. By hearing the Authorized Version, a congregation is connected to their trusted and cherished heritage. The scriptures they hear quoted and preached from the pulpit are the same they can read devotionally in private and as families. They immediately recognize the language spoken from the pulpit as the same as that contained in the confessions and catechisms which they study, memorize, and teach to their children. Further, the Scripture proofs in the confessions coincide with what is preached from the pulpit. After the sermon, they can also turn to one of the classic Reformed commentaries for further study, and they will find a blessed and happy continuity.

In many confessional churches, the Lord's Prayer is recited corporately. When congregations make use of the traditional text, no one need worry about stopping short of the blessed conclusion (the doxology of Matthew 6:13b), relegated, for example, to a footnote in the English Standard Version. When they catechize their children, asking, "What doth the conclusion to the Lord's prayer teach us?", parents can be confident that the text used at church confirms what their children are taught at home, namely:

> The conclusion of the Lord's prayer (which is, *For thine is the kingdom, and the power, and the glory, for ever, Amen*) teacheth us to take our encouragement in prayer from God only, and in our prayers to praise him, ascribing kingdom, power, and glory to him. And, in testimony of our desire, and assurance to be heard, we say, *Amen* (WSC, 107; Baptist Catechism, 114).

The Received Text is the text of Reformed church members.

Conclusion

Although there are many reasons why I preach from the Received

Text, one of the most important is because the Received Text *is* the Reformed text. Not only the text of one or two prominent Reformed theologians, but the text of all "Reformed catholicism," that is, the text universally received and used by the men who established, synthesized, codified, and taught the Reformed faith. I find that is not only the safest and most faithful practice of confessional churches to make use of the traditional text, but it is also the necessary conclusion of adopting the Reformed heritage. As Reformed Christians, we must acknowledge that the Received Text is the text of our forefathers and their theology, and thus it should be the text our Pastors preach from and our members read. It is my prayer that all who love and hold to the Reformed confessions would return to the text which made those confessions possible.

Dane Johannsson (undergraduate studies Moody Bible Institute, and ongoing study with Puritan Reformed Theological Seminary) planted Agros Reformed Baptist Church in Mesa, Arizona and currently serves as pastoral intern at Reformation Orthodox Presbyterian Church in Apache Junction, Arizona. He and his wife have three children.

Acknowledgement: The editors express their gratitude to Dane for his invaluable assistance in the early development of this anthology.

11

Perspectives from the Pew

Howie W. Owen Jones

The Pew, Pastor, and Professor

I have the privilege of sitting in the pew each Lord's Day at a faithful church, so this chapter is admittedly unique as it modifies the thrust of this book to: *Why I desire to be preached to from the Received Text.* The issue of the text and transmission of holy Scripture is vital for those of us in the pew, not just for pastors and professors who also love God's sacred Word—because the issue goes to the heart of *Sola Scriptura*, biblical authority, inspiration, canon, and doctrinal fidelity. It impacts us all!

A lot is at stake when a churchgoer is asked, "Please take your Bible and open it to..." Yet, it seems most people in the pew give little thought to their Bible's underlying text, assuming it to be exactly what its cover declares it to be, the Holy Bible. This was once my mindset, but one day a statement I heard concerning a denial of part of God's Word gave rise to a burning question: Did I have a solid and supportable understanding concerning the text backing the Bible version I used? I had to acknowledge that I did not, and that led me to ask more questions. How could I be certain that the Bible version I used, or a new Bible version promoted by a publisher, was authentic?

Question, Then Deny

The battle for God's Word shows itself at the very beginning in Genesis 3:1-4, where the following pattern may be observed: first, question and challenge what God has said, and, second, drive to the real purpose which is a denial of God's Word, in whole or in part. A rejection of what God has said is always Satan's grand purpose. Today textual denial remains a subtle ploy, often innocently re-circulated in seminaries and pulpits, eventually filtering down to the pew. This relationship promotes a self-sustaining modern Bible industry. A sort of "Text Pharma" keeps the machine well-oiled in the background, which is especially evident in the West, where consumers can afford to purchase "better" Bibles from publishers skilled at marketing "updated" texts.

Above all this, infinitely and eternally, is God. His immutable decrees providentially executed in time and history are never dependent upon man! We can therefore contend with all confidence and authority that the Scriptures are not subject to man's "better judgements," "approximations," or "consensus reconstructions." The Word of God is forever settled (Psalm 119:89), pure (Proverbs 30:5), divinely breathed (2 Timothy 3:16), and it abides forever (Matthew 24:35; 1 Peter 1:23-25). He upholds his every word.

On such a foundation, I will seek to present several primary reasons why I desire to hear preaching from the Received Text (i.e. Textus Receptus or TR). I will contend that the TR is the providentially preserved text of the Word of God, faithfully kept pure in all ages by its Author, the I AM.

Textual Worldview and Scriptural Authority

The first reason I desire to hear preaching from the Received Text is because God has committed himself to keeping his Word pure, and we must therefore respond accordingly. In contrast, the Critical Text which lies behind many newer English Bible versions is a product of modern textual criticism and does not hold conceptually or practically to this providential reality. Enlightenment thinking has significantly influenced contemporary mainstream textual criticism. It generally supposes that the text of Scripture has been corrupted and that the *autographs* (i.e., original inspired manuscripts) must be reconstructed to an approximation. This textual worldview results in uncertainty and instability, because the resulting text is in a continual state of flux. Of course, such a view runs contrary to the scriptures (Psalm 119:89; Proverbs 30:5; Matthew 24:35; 1 Peter 1:23-25). It also contradicts the Westminster Confession of Faith, the Savoy Declaration, and the London Baptist Confession of Faith of 1689. In chapter 1 paragraph 8 these confessions rightly assert that the scriptures were "immediately inspired by God," which speaks of the *autographs*. These are not extant, but "by his singular care and providence [they have been] kept pure in all ages." This confession declares that the transmission and providential history of the *apographs* (copies of the originals) have been divinely preserved (cf. John Owen, *Collected Works*, Vol. 16, 473-477).

A comparison can be made to a teeter-totter. On one side, the Received Text tips toward certainty as it feels the weight of providential preservation. On the other side, the Critical Text tips toward uncertainty, as it gives weight to man's approximations, modifications, and ever-changing determinations. Your textual worldview will cause you to lean toward one side or the other.

Let me also suggest a "Text Criticism Key" which I believe can be helpful in unlocking difficulties related to textual questions: If we embrace the Bibliology represented in the opening chapter of the classic Protestant and Reformed Confessions as the foundation of our view of Scripture, we will not be carried away into questioning the sacred text or ultimately denying it.

Applying this "Key" helps one place the complex details of the "Text Critical Monster" into perspective. While the topic of textual criticism might seem philosophical and academic, the position one takes will always have practical effect. For example, making use of the Text Criticism Key, it can be observed that some churches confess the Reformed standards, such as the Westminster Larger and Shorter Catechisms. These standards affirm the doxology of the Lord's Prayer in Matthew 6:13b (WSC, 107). At the same time, however, these same churches may use modern Bible versions which omit the doxology. This is perplexing and contradictory. The Text Criticism Key is refreshingly directive. If only such churches would make use of this "Key" they would affirm the traditional text of Scripture, insisting upon infallible Biblical truth, over against man's reason and fallibility.

Uncertainties in the Critical Text

The second reason I desire to hear preaching from the Received Text is because there are many uncertainties in the Critical Text. It was birthed out of Enlightenment thinking that led to a New Testament text based primarily on two uncial codices *Sinaiticus* and *Vaticanus* (the former discovered in the nineteenth century and the latter rejected by the Reformers). Most modern New Testament Bible versions are based on these texts.

The modern method is based upon what scholars call reasoned eclecticism. The term "eclectic" is misleading, though its adjunct term "reasoned" is not. This text relies primarily on just two heavy-weight manuscripts and, to a far lesser extent, upon other minor manuscripts, including papyri. The stable TR and the unstable Critical Text differ in thousands of places. Verses are questioned and even removed in the Critical Text. Some argue that no doctrine has been compromised by the differences, but this sort of thinking ignores the importance of the text and its relationship with doctrine. One could remove the texts of Genesis 1:1 or John 3:16 and argue that no doctrine is compromised when considering the Bible as a whole, but this is unpersuasive. Tampering with the text of Scripture necessarily affects the stability, integrity, and authority of Scripture. In contrast, the Received Text is consistently and tenaciously stable, being based on witnesses that:

...are nearly consistent, not only with one another, but also with the vast majority of manuscripts of the Greek New Testament which were available to scholars of the Reformation and which are available to scholars today.... Therefore, regardless of which edition of the Textus Receptus one chooses, he is getting a New Testament which represents the majority of manuscripts available then and now. His Critical Greek Text does not ("The Validity of the Textus Receptus," *Quarterly Record*, Number 629, October to December 2019, 12).

Is the Bible a Hypothetical Reconstruction?

The third reason 1 desire to hear preaching from the Received Text is because it does not require text "adjustments" and "corrections" by man-made standards of approximated or hypothetical textual reconstruction. The Critical Text now relies on computer algorithms, referred to as the *Coherence-Based Genealogical Method* (CBGM) (cf. Jeffrey T. Riddle, "The Coherence-Based Genealogical Method: The Newest 'New' Method," *Quarterly Record*, Issue No. 635 [2021]: 12-19). The results are being published in the *Editio Critica Maior* (ECM), a significant critical edition of the Greek New Testament, projected to be completed by 2030. According to the German Bible Society website, the ECM initiative holds that "the existing text required extensive modification" resulting in a "hypothetical reconstruction" of the text. This is a staggering admission.

At the core of the Critical Text worldview is the belief that man's enlightened reason should be exercised over the infallible, stable, and pure God-breathed text of holy writ. With this assumption, how is it possible that doctrine and preaching will not be affected or influenced when man's reason usurps scriptural authority? The Received Text, on the other hand, is not a hypothetical reconstruction. It is not the product of man's fallible reason, but the result of the providential preservation of the infallible God. A text which requires extensive modification every few years denies the doctrine of providential preservation and should be rejected by the church.

Variants and the Pew

I have attended public church services where people stared at their Bibles in bewilderment because the Pastor read a verse that did not appear in their version, or, worse still, because the Pastor's Bible skipped a verse that did appear in their Bible. At such times, I have wondered what negative influence this could have on a new or weak believer. Similarly, when a Pastor brings attention to variants in the text, those in the pew generally have little or no idea what he is talking about. Rather than offering clarification, he unwittingly introduces doubt about the text or passage. This is serious. It undermines the scriptures, casts doubt on the Word, and leaves listeners without adequate answers.

Without doubt, Critical Text variants foster confusion and uncertainty in the pew. Scripture authenticates itself. It is its own divine standard of absolute certainty. The Received Text, which was providentially recognized and affirmed at the time of the Reformation and the invention of the printing press, has all the marks of a text divinely preserved and kept pure in all ages. It was the Received Text that was faithfully translated into many languages and was universally received by God's people during the greatest revival since Pentecost. Unlike the Critical Text, there has never been a need for seismic modifications of the Received Text.

Most of us in the pew are not prepared to digest or make sense of text-variant sound bites. When a Pastor unintentionally undermines the authenticity of the text of Scripture, he unwittingly risks undermining the faith and confidence of his hearers in the Word of God. Of course, this is a true Pastor's worst nightmare. This would not happen if Pastors embraced the Received Text as the authoritative and providentially preserved Word of God.

A Brotherly Appeal

My appeal from the pew is that my dear brothers who are Pastors and Professors would preach and teach from the Received Text.

By this, I mean that text, as generally found in the majority of manuscript witnesses (sometimes called the Byzantine text-type), which served as the basis of the printed Received Text (Masoretic text of the Hebrew OT and the *Textus Receptus* of the Greek NT). This text is the one affirmed in the Protestant and Reformed Confessional Standards. It is undeniably the providentially preserved text of the Word of God, kept pure in all ages by its Author, the I AM.

These are not easy things to work through, but they are vital. May our Lord and Saviour Jesus Christ increase our love to him, to his people and the lost, and toward *all aspects* of Holy Scripture! "Forever settled in the heav'ns, Thy Word, O Lord, shall firmly stand; Exceeding broad is thy command, And in perfection shall endure" (*Trinity Hymnal*, no. 54).

Howie W. Owen Jones (B.A. Trinity Western University; M.B.A. Royal Roads University) is a small business owner and Deacon at Surrey Reformed Baptist Church in British Columbia, Canada, where he resides with his wife and the youngest of their four children.

12

Why I Read and Preach from the TR and AV

Trevor Kirkland

The Westminster Confession of Faith states that God gave his word originally in Hebrew and Greek. Because every believer is not able to read "these original tongues... therefore they are to be translated" (WCF, 1.8). What cannot be overlooked here is that the Westminster divines believed they had the true and authentic text, that it was preserved and kept pure in all ages, and that it was authoritative and to be referred to in all controversies. The result of this theological conviction is of fundamental importance. If the church has the true, pure, and authentic text, then we do not need to go looking for it. Further, it remains unchanging, reliable, and authoritative for believers and preachers. Having been a preacher for over thirty years, the following is why I shall continue to preach from this text.

First, a Bible Based upon a True Text

When the NIV first came out there were many astonishing claims
made in the footnotes. For example, we read "the earliest manuscripts do not have...," and many were fooled by this sleight of hand.
God never promised to preserve the *manuscripts* upon which the
text was written; rather, he promised to preserve the *words*. This
is an important principle which is too often overlooked. Consider
the following reality. Roman Catholicism teaches that the "Church"
will tell us what the Bible is. This claim was clearly rejected by the
Reformers, who insisted that the Bible was self-attesting. Here too,
many Protestants are confused about the relationship between
church and Bible. As William Whitaker makes clear, Rome says that
the authority of the Bible depends upon the authority of the church
(cf. *Disputations*, 276). By contrast, our position is that Scripture has
authority in itself and thus the role of the church is to recognize
its authenticity and then proclaim and defend it as a "notary" or
"champion" (*Disputations*, 283).

Yet something odd has happened in contemporary evangelical
circles. In the place of Rome, evangelicals have put the academy in
the belief that it will provide to us the true Word of God. As a result,
translations have multiplied, all claiming the best academic credentials. Yet, at no time has the church ever decided that academics
should have this role. To the contrary, this is a doctrinal issue for
every believer in the pew to consider. The question is simple: Has
God spoken? If so, where is his Word? The answer is that God has
caused his inspired Word to be written down and has kept that
Word. That is the Word we need, and that is the Word we must
have: the preserved Word of God. We have every confidence that

the church has always had that Word, that from that preserved Word in Hebrew and Greek the best vernacular translations have come, including the best English translation to date, the Authorized Version (AV).

Here then is the fundamental issue for every believer in the pew: Does the preacher before me, believe that he has the pure, true, authentic preserved Word of God? By using a modern Bible based upon an eclectic text, that preacher does *not* so believe, however much he may shout and argue for his preferred modern Bible.

Second, a Bible That Is an Honest Translation

It is essential that preachers and people know the Bible in their hand is a reliable translation from the authentic text. It is astonishing then to come across translations which confuse or falsify the text.

One example of translational confusion is found in the NKJV's rendering of 2 Kings 23:29. It reports that the king of Egypt "went to the aid" of the king of Assyria, while in the parallel passage in 2 Chronicles 35:20, it reads that the king "came up to fight against" the Assyrians. So which is true? By contrast, the AV rendering is consistent, having the king in opposition to the Assyrians in both passages. Any preacher using the NKJV is effectively conveying to the people that contradictions may exist in the Word of God.

Another example of potential falsification is found in Micah 7:19. The NKJV reads, "You will cast all our sins," but the footnote states that the literal reading is "their" sins. This is, of course, the precise reading we have in the AV. So why the change? The footnote does not explain. However, if we consult the NRSV, the footnote explains that the reading is following the LXX, Syriac, and Vulgate.

In other words, the NKJV footnote is misleading.

Third, Preachers Need a Reliable Translation

Over the years, I have lost count of the complaints by commentators regarding the scripture text they are using for their commentary, whether it be the NIV or the ESV. Preachers naturally purchase numerous commentaries, and these reference works often form the bulk of their library. After a short while, they soon discover how unreliable these modern works can be. Consider the following examples:

Philip Ryken, in his commentary on Galatians 4:1, says that the ESV reading *owner of everything* misses the point, because the heir does not own it, but the father does. The AV rightly reads *lord of all*. Had Ryken used the text of the AV there would not have been a problem.

Timothy George in his commentary on Galatians at 2:16 states that the NIV totally ignores the Greek text and translates the Septuagint instead of Paul.

David Peterson states regarding Acts 20:17 that the TNIV obscures the forcefulness of the Greek. The sad reality is that commentaries based upon the ESV, NIV, and TNIV cause writers numerous problems. Such problems would not arise, if they insisted upon using a translation based upon the true and authentic text of Scripture.

Fourth, Preachers Need a Conservative Translation

As noted already, our preference for a translation of the TR is the AV. We are not claiming perfection for the AV. Granted, it does have some blemishes and imperfections; however, the translators were not interested in being "contemporary." Ironically, this has become a common criticism (i.e., that it uses "archaic" language) when, in fact, some of its language was already archaic in 1611!

Anyone who takes the trouble to read the *Preface* or the *Translators to the Reader*, will notice a difference in style when compared to the biblical text. As Nicholson states, "it has an air of irreproachable authority. Its language was the language spoken by God" (*God's Secretaries*, 232-3). This conservatism may be observed in the translators' avoidance of colloquial or slang terms common in their day.

For example, in Titus 2:10 there was the suggested translation of *no filchers*, and it was rejected for *not purloining*. "Filch" was an Elizabethan slang word dating from 1561. By contrast, "purloin" dates from 1440. The English of the AV was meant to serve the original meaning, not replace it. It speaks in its Master's voice as opposed to the language you hear in the street. It was more important to make English godly than to make the words of God into some fashionable prose. What a contrast with modern translations which are forever being updated to suit the prevailing culture and fashion. Such a changeable and moveable text undermines the fixed truth of God in the mind of the hearer.

Fifth, Preachers Need a Memorable Translation

The AV was "appointed to be read" because at the center of Protestant worship is the Holy Bible. It is to be read, sung, prayed, and preached. Even if people forget the sermon, they will still recall the Word of God taught to them. The AV is without doubt a memorable translation of the inspired Word. As Miles Smith, author of the *Translators to the Reader*, makes plain, "Add hereunto, that niceness in words was always counted the next step to trifling." In other words, they were not interested in producing something nice but something accurate. Since it was appointed to be read, the translators gathered to hear it being read aloud. One member of the committee was appointed to read the translation, while the rest listened in silence until there was an interruption. The problem raised was discussed in numerous languages, the fathers were cited in support or against, and so it continued until the right word was chosen. Nicholson writes that the translators made a ceremony of the Word. From the AV then comes an entire library of memorable phrases, words and sentences such as: "For mine eyes have seen thy salvation," "Behold I stand at the door and knock," and "For unto us a child is born, unto us a son is a given."

Sixth, an International Bible
The AV was translated not by *ad hoc* committees but by appointed companies, the point being that it was not limited to one country, but for the entire English speaking world. We should be appalled that there is a specific American Bible, or British Bible, or any other national Bible. When we consider that there is neither Jew nor Greek, then the Bible should be the same for all who speak the same language, a single Bible. That was the aim of the translators. Sadly the church has been fractured at its heart by the plethora of niche Bibles. Not only national Bibles but Women's Bibles, Teen's Bibles, Married Couple's Bibles, etc. This is an appalling abuse of the Word of God for financial benefit. By using the AV, the believer and the preacher is, at once, reading the same word, hearing the same word,

and trusting the same word.

Seventh, the Preacher Must Have a Permanent Bible

The reason there are so many texts and versions is because there is an entire industry geared to producing newer Bibles. Chronological snobbery reigns, but underlying this is the atheistic view that we do not actually have the full Word of God, but only an approximation to it. The Majority Text position, for example, is entirely unreliable depending as it does upon how many manuscripts are currently extant. At any moment, a new discovery may alter the text. The majority position is thus unreliable and unsettled.

Some will here raise the question of variants. Firstly, within the Received Text tradition there are very few, and they are often noted in the margin of the AV. Secondly, where the translators were unsure as to the precise translation they gave an alternative in the margin. We see this in Psalm 150:4 where the text reads *dance*, but in the margin *pipe* is offered as an alternative. In their integrity and honesty the translators make it clear that they were unable to decide which reading is correct. At the same time, they did not need to go looking for the text, since they were wholly confident that they held the text in their hand. They did not need to wait for any further discoveries. A permanent text is essential to the pulpit ministry.

Every time then, as I ascend into the pulpit, I do so knowing that I have the true, authentic text of Scripture translated into English by the cream of believing scholarship, surpassing much of what we have today. A Bible for all the church, not the few. A Bible that has shaped literature, art, science, and, above all, theology, Christianity, and the church.

Trevor Kirkland (B.A. Hons., Dip.Th.) *is Assistant Editor of* The Witness, *Board Member of the Trinitarian Bible Society* (Canada and Australia), *lecturer in Church History and Principles, and Pastor of the Ballyclare & Doagh Free Church* (Continuing), *where he resides with his wife. He has four children and three grandchildren.*

13

Hank, James, and Me: My Journey to the Received Text

Brett Mahlen

My path to preaching from the Received Text (TR) was not a straight line; it was a roundabout journey. Some would say that I "fetched a compass" in my route. I am presently a Pastor and professor to inmates in a maximum-security prison where I engage in ministerial duties, including meaningful apologetics. I also preach Lord's Day by Lord's Day in a Reformed church.

I still remember where I was in the late 1990s when I first heard Dr. James White on Hank Hanegraaff's *The Bible Answer Man Broadcast* talking about White's recent book, *The King James Only Controversy*. I was recently converted to Christ at the time, and I was drinking in as much Bible teaching and doctrine as I could find, and Hanegraaff had been satisfying my thirst. On that day I was fascinated by every word these two men said, whether they were talking about the KJV itself, manuscripts, history, or taking calls. Desiderius Erasmus and other names seemed to roll off their tongues effortlessly even though I had never heard them before. I knew on that day that I needed to learn what these men knew.

I continued as a Hanegraaff listener for many years, and I went on to read a few of White's books, his articles, and I benefited from his debates. Both men taught me much about truth and error. I did not automatically believe what they taught, I checked it out for myself (as they taught me to do).

As a young Christian, I was vehemently opposed to Calvinism. In an effort to bolster my arguments, I decided to buy Norman Geisler's book *Chosen But Free*, but when I went to buy it its rebuttal came up, White's *The Potter's Freedom: A Defense of the Reformation and a Rebuttal of Norman Geisler's Chosen But Free*. I read both books and in the end I realized that I could be an Arminian no longer. God used White to open my eyes to God's sovereignty; I am grateful for God's kindness to me in that.

In the spring of 2001, I wrote an email to James White, and he wrote me back. I was amazed that he had written back to a nobody like me, but I was also struck by how long and thorough his answer was. He clearly took my question seriously, even though I was a stranger, and it was a private email.

While attending college, I joined a Reformed church, and the Pastor explained the doctrine of providential preservation to me. He explained the issue of Bible manuscripts, the *so-called* earlier and better manuscripts, the story of how allegedly one manuscript was found in the trash and saved from burning, etc. I left college with a conviction that God had preserved his word, but as I reflect back now my understanding of these issues was not deep.

In seminary I needed to take *New Testament Introduction*; this class had Bruce Metzger and Bart Ehrman's *The Text of the New Testament: Its Transmission, Corruption, and Restoration* (underlining mine) as a textbook. It seemed that this class armed students with quick "facts" to discredit the Textus Receptus like: "Erasmus introduced 1 John 5:7 into the text on a dare," "Erasmus only had access to a few copies of the Greek New Testament," and "Erasmus back-translated the last six verses of Revelation from Latin into Greek," etc. Needing to stay on track with my studies (and having a job outside of seminary), I did not have time to investigate these claims, and I was forced to move on to other issues. I resolved that other than the two large disputed sections (Mark 16 and John 8) and the sixteen other verses not found in modern Bibles, the rest of the NT was pretty settled, and I would just have to live with that.

It was also during that time that I was introduced to the English Standard Version (ESV) of the Bible. I believed having lots of versions was extremely helpful to get back to the original Greek and Hebrew, so I added the ESV to my list of approved versions. I gently advocated for the ESV during my first pastorate (which lasted six years). The church had the New American Standard Bible (NASB) in the pews, so I ordinarily read from it in worship, but I grew weary of it because of its wooden literalism, its word choices, and its clunky feel when reading. It seemed that the Bible should sound more beautiful, and I thought the ESV sounded much better.

Reading both the ESV and NASB week in and week out along with the two critical Greek New Testaments (United Bible Societies and Nestle Aland) and also *A Reader's Greek New Testament* (a Greek text which was "reverse engineered" [their words, p. 10] to conform to the NIV) caused me to see that there was a lot more that was unsettled in the Greek New Testament than I had previously thought.

I began to dig deeper into the study of textual criticism. I began to read the Metzger/Ehrman book more slowly than I was able to do in seminary. That book took on a devotional tone to me. I rejoiced in the overthrow of the TR, as I was encouraged to do from page 170 and onward. I could find no advocates of the Received Text who were academically qualified or competent in Greek. For years I had listened to White's debates with KJV-Onlyists like Gail Riplinger, and White seemed to defeat them all, usually rising above their personal attacks, and sometimes the debates were downright hilarious (especially the Riplinger debate). I was a walking contradiction, unsettled in my view of the text, yet rejoicing in the downfall of the Received Text, and seeking to gain more knowledge of the unsettled nature of the text.

As I continued to read the modern versions, more doubt began to set in my mind. The translational differences, but especially the textual possibilities in the apparatus of the Greek New Testaments, began to bother me more than ever. Previously, I had been able to ignore the differences because I was just an avid Bible reading layman. In ministry, however, I had to preach the text, but before I could preach the text, I had to be sure what it was. Yet sometimes I was unsure. I had internal struggles because of the unsettled text.

There were many Orthodox and one Romish church in the town where I lived, and while I was offended by their errors, their belief that the ancient creeds were still relevant fascinated me. These churches provided first-hand opportunities for studying forms of

Christianity that did not have a high regard for *sola scriptura*.

Providentially, God called me out of my first pastorate to minister in a prison context. Much of the work there would be apologetic, and many things began ruminating in my mind. Most of the inmates were African American and used the King James Version, but I used the ESV. I was listening to White and Hanegraaff again, and I was being edified.

My heart was broken as I heard the news that on Easter Sunday, 2017, Mr. Hanegraaff was chrismated in a Greek Orthodox church. Although I never took Hank to be infallible, I often found his opinion to be well-informed. He usually encouraged people to research topics for themselves rather than simply to adopt his opinion. I had a hard time respecting his conversion to Eastern Orthodoxy, but I think I might understand it better now. Hank went from atheism to evangelicalism, and therefore did not have a church background which gave much emphasis to ecclesiastical history. Like many people who leave evangelicalism, it may be that he believes evangelicalism is non-historical, as Ed Setzer and others argue (cf. blog article at christianitytoday.com, "Hank Hanegraaff's Switch to Eastern Orthodoxy, Why People Make Such Changes, and Four Ways Evangelicals Might Respond"). I also appreciated White's critique of Hanegraaff's conversion.

Almost twenty years earlier, however, White had assured Hanegraaff on his show that the text of the Bible was not a sure thing. The implication of White's teaching about the Bible was that it had been corrupted by additions from the "orthodox" who allegedly added the ending to Mark, the woman caught in adultery in John 8, and sixteen other verses being either added or corrupted (e.g., I

Timothy 3:16). Both men readily told listeners, if I may summarize, that due to the vast information and resources we have today, all these "uninspired additions" were removed by the nineteenth century revision committee, and it is only traditionalists and conspiracy theorists who want to keep such verses in the Bible.

With no historic confession and no Bible that was on a sure footing, it makes sense that Hank would leave evangelicalism in search of a church with stronger historical foundations. Maybe if White had assured Hanegraaff that God's Word had been kept pure in all ages (as Owen and Turretin had in the seventeenth century), rather than corrupted by the orthodox, a different result may have taken place. Hanegraaff says he converted because of *theosis*, but these matters are always more complex than one issue.

While previously disappointed by the caliber of men who defended the TR, I eventually discovered defenders who actually knew Greek and Hebrew and had credentials. Dr. Theodore P. Letis was my introduction to such men, and he introduced me to William Burgon and Edward F. Hills. I was familiar with James White's criticisms of these men, but I had not read them for myself, so I began to pore over these men's works and I was amazed. They did not have the foolishness that I found so common in KJV-Onlyists, and it became ever clearer that these men were not so much advocating for a particular English version as they were standing for the catholic faith and the catholic Bible as it was handed down from the Apostles. The term "catholic" means "universal" as was reflected in the fact that one was Lutheran, one was a Anglican, and one was Presbyterian. It became clear to me that these men were not inventing something new, but they were defending the Reformation view itself, demonstrated especially by John Owen, Francis Turretin, William Whitaker, and the framers of the Protestant confessions.

In my reading I discovered two biographies of the KJV translators (one by Alexander McClure, the other by Gustavus Paine). We live in a time with many brilliant people. I have met, sat under, and interacted with many of them, but if half the things contained in these books are true, then the KJV translators were head and shoulders above anyone alive today. Brilliant as many men are today, I do not believe many, if any, would have the credentials to sit on the KJV translation committee. The meetings would be mostly in Latin, and I do not believe many within Protestantism have that capacity with the language. In addition, the modern standards of proficiency in Hebrew and Greek are not up to the seventeenth century standard. McClure says:

> Imagine our greenish contemporaries shut up with an Andrews, a Reynolds, a Ward, and a Bois, comparing notes on the meaning of the original Scriptures! It would soon be found, that all the aid our poor moderns could render would be in snuffing the candles (*Translators Revived*, 179).

Burgon, Hills, and Letis have written worthy books. For Burgon, I recommend *Revision Revised* and *Inspiration and Interpretation*. Hills' *King James Version Defended* also deserves high praise. Hills was a man with the fighting spirit of Machen, the academic rigor of a Westminster Theological Seminary graduate and two Ivy League degrees (from a time in which the Ivy League was impressive), a credentialed textual critic, a philosopher, and he was seeking to apply

Cornelius Van Til's presuppositionalism to textual criticism. I found myself at home in much of Dr. Hills' thinking and wondered where his writings had been all my Christian life.

Further, I recommend Letis' few lectures that are available online, his master's thesis, and his book *The Ecclesiastical Text*. The latter volume shows in chapter one how Warfield had moved the Reformed focus from infallible *apographs* to inerrant *autographs*. Chapter five argues that modern Bibles contain a heretical reading in John 1:18. Chapter eight provides the history of the TR and shows, ironically, how Independent Fundamentalist Baptists became advocates of the KJV, even though they are divorced from the history of that version; meanwhile, Reformation Protestants abandoned the KJV and the TR. I learned that there was more depth than first appeared when I used to listen to James White's dismissals of these men.

I also discovered the podcast *Word Magazine* and came to appreciate Jeff Riddle's critiques of White, Ehrman, Wallace, and others. The ending of episode #54 on *The Comma Johanneum and the Papyri* made me nearly fall off my chair.

When I finally began using the KJV in my prison ministry, I felt like I had caught up to the inmates. Most of them read the KJV with understanding even though many came from poorly-run urban schools with historically poor test scores. These men in prison actually had dictionaries, and used them! It has been a delight to preach and teach from the same version they have in their hands, and they have appreciated it as well. In seminary classes, I have also taught them about God's promise to preserve his Word, and I have encouraged them with believing, Protestant, textual criticism.

During the coronavirus situation in 2020-21 I was unable to

enter the prison so I found an interim Pastorate at a small church while I waited for the prison to open again. I tried an experiment: preaching from the KJV without explicitly arguing for it. That church has grown to appreciate the version very much, and there has been no opposition to it.

In the Reformed Faith, especially that contained in the WCF, we have all that is good in the Council of Nicaea and the early church but without the debris that accumulated in later centuries, like icons, incense, prayers to saints, prayers for the dead, and other man-made corruptions. I would argue that the Westminster Standards are an exposition of the best of the Patristic era, especially Nicaea and Chalcedon. If Hanegraaff had been exposed to this, perhaps he would have embraced the Reformation rather than Eastern Orthodoxy.

Some TR advocates like to insult James White, but I do not find that helpful. I do believe Dr. Riddle defeated Dr. White in the two debates of October 2020, however, just because I disagree with Dr. White or believe he lost a debate does not make him my enemy. I still benefit from his books and his debates against Romanists, cultists, and Muslims. I appreciate his stand against wokeism. All men have feet of clay, and I learn from a wide variety of men with whom I may disagree on some issues.

The sixteenth and seventeenth century Protestants were correct that God has kept his Word pure!

Brett Mahlen (B.A. Colorado State University; M.Div. Westminster Theological Seminary; S.T.M. Trinity School for Ministry; D.Min. Reformed Presbyterian Theological Seminary) teaches at Divine Hope Reformed Bible Seminary and is associate Pastor of Covenant Orthodox Presbyterian Church in Orland Park, Illinois, where he resides with his wife and daughter.

14

Scripture Identified Scripture

Robert McCurley

The first recorded words of Satan are, "Yea, hath God said...?" (Genesis 3:1). In his opening salvo, the devil focused his attack on undermining the Word of God and nothing has changed since that time. He has continued to employ this same perverse tactic throughout the ages, all with the sustained aim of derailing souls. Four thousand years later, Paul was still warning the Corinthians, "But I fear, lest by any means, as the serpent beguiled Eve through his subtilty, so your minds should be corrupted from the simplicity that is in Christ" (2 Corinthians 11:3).

When it comes to assailing the scriptures, Satan employs a limited arsenal. He can attempt to take away the Bible by limiting physical access to the scriptures. He can tempt men who have the Bible to turn away their hearts and minds from the truths and doctrines it teaches. He can also seek to undermine men's confidence in the Bible. Given these varied assaults, we are warned to watch, to stand, and to resist.

I grew up within a Bible-believing Christian home that prized the gospel and promoted godliness. My parents nurtured their children in a spiritual environment that cultivated the fear of the Lord. When it came to Bible versions, however, we lacked clarity. Like most of those around us, confusion seemed to abound. Consequently, we learned to eat from what might be considered a "translation smorgasbord." Both our family and the congregations we attended drew from a wide array of translations. While we had limited exposure to the Authorized (King James) Version within that greater milieu, it was set alongside many other Bible versions that always received the place of primacy. To compound the problem, no one furnished us with the reasons behind particular translations, nor provided the tools and resources to decipher the differences and to assess their faithfulness.

Now a few decades later, I have served Christ in the gospel ministry for over twenty years. In my personal studies, our family worship, and in all aspects of my pastoral ministry, I confine myself to the Received Text in the original languages and to the English language translation based on that text, known as the Authorized (King James) Version. This present volume seeks to supply an answer to the question: Why? Why do I choose to preach from the Received Text? Clearly, my upbringing, previous preference, or ecclesiastical tradition are not the reason I choose to preach from the Received Text. I did not grow up using the Authorized (King James) Version of the Bible; I came to this practice in mature adulthood.

What, then, is the answer? I preach from the Received Text out of personal conviction and commitment to biblical principle. *I believe that the scriptures identify the text of Scripture.* God alone supplies his Word, specifies his Word, and sustains his Word. And he reveals that to us in the Bible. We ought to answer questions about the text and translation of Scripture based on the Bible itself. God has not left the Church to the whim of computer geeks who must develop software and run algorithms in order to inform us what text should be included in our Bibles. Likewise, the believer does not depend upon unbelieving methodology, nor may he employ the world's depraved assumptions in grappling with textual questions regarding God's Word. We must look to the Lord and turn to our Bibles on matters of such enormous magnitude. The church of the living God, the pillar and ground of the truth, must receive the Word that God provides.

God reveals in his Word that he will providentially preserve the text of Scripture throughout all ages. Jesus asserted this truth in the Sermon on the Mount in Matthew 5:18, "For verily I say unto you, Till heaven and earth pass, one jot or one tittle shall in no wise pass from the law, till all be fulfilled." As Christ proceeds to affirm, this preservation remains necessary for the whole Word to be taught, applied and obeyed, and he issues a sober warning to any who curtail in the least degree the revelation we have received from him. Jesus was drawing upon what the Law and the Prophets themselves had taught. In the Law, we read, "... but those things which are revealed belong unto us and to our children for ever, that we may do all the words of this law" (Deuteronomy 29:29). Further, in the Prophets, we are told, "As for me, this is my covenant with them, saith the

LORD; My spirit that is upon thee, and my words which I have put in thy mouth, shall not depart out of thy mouth, nor out of the mouth of thy seed, nor out of the mouth of thy seed's seed, saith the LORD, from henceforth and for ever" (Isaiah 59:21). The scriptures identify the text of Scripture, and they make clear that God's Word will be recognized and received as that which he himself preserves throughout all ages (cf. Psalm 12:6-7, 119:160; Isaiah 40:8; 1 Peter 1:25).

As a Presbyterian minister committed to the Reformed faith, I affirmed in my ministerial vows the following:

> Do you sincerely own and believe the whole doctrine con-
> tained in the [Westminster] Confession of Faith... to be
> founded upon the Word of God; and do you acknowledge
> the same as the confession of your faith; and will you firmly
> and constantly adhere thereto, and to the utmost of your
> power assert, maintain, and defend the same...?

Among other fundamental doctrines, Westminster Confession of Faith 1.8 states that the Holy Scriptures "... being immediately inspired by God, and, *by his singular care and providence kept pure in all ages*, are therefore authentical..." [emphasis mine].

This biblical doctrine excludes the critical and eclectic texts of Scripture and all translations based upon them (e.g., ESV, NIV, NASB, etc.), as they draw upon manuscripts unavailable and unrecognized by the church for centuries. Utilizing such manuscripts appears to deny in practice and principle that God has providentially preserved his Word. Instead, this implies that the Lord left his church without the pure Word of God over an extended period, contrary to his infallible promise. It should be disconcerting to see allegedly confessional churches in the Reformed heritage departing from this confessional standard.

God also reveals in his Word that we must recognize and reject all perversions of the text of Scripture—hence emphasizing the principle of "kept pure." Perversion can take place through the twisting of Scripture's teaching, which leads to the destruction of those who distort God's Word (2 Peter 3:16), but it can also occur through the purposeful alteration of the text of Scripture. For this, God issues a terrifying imprecation:

> For I testify unto every man that heareth the words of the prophecy of this book, If any man shall add unto these things, God shall add unto him the plagues that are written in this book: And if any man shall take away from the words of the book of this prophecy, God shall take away his part out of the book of life, and out of the holy city, and from the things which are written in this book (Revelation 22:18-19).

For this reason, the ancient scribes placed the highest possible priority on meticulous and stringent accuracy in copying and transmitting the scriptures. The Received Text reflects the fruit of this tireless and faithful labor. For example, whereas the Received Text, reflecting 97% of manuscripts says, "God was manifest in the flesh" (1 Timothy 3:16), the modern critical texts, drawing on corrupt manuscripts from a region rife with Arian heresy, delete the word "God," thus undermining the divine glory of Christ.

A further example includes the ending of the Lord's Prayer in Matthew 6:13. The Westminster Assembly took a stand by including this text in the Larger and Shorter Catechisms, which reflects the stance of Protestant and Reformed confessions and Bible translations throughout Europe. It is well beyond the scope of this single chapter to multiply similar examples. We merely note that the Bible calls us to affirm that God superintends the preservation of the *purity* of his Word.

What authority guides us in recognizing and receiving the text of Scripture? It is not autonomous man. In all controversies, we must subject ourselves to the authority of God in the scriptures. In a dispute over the resurrection, we read: "Jesus answered and said unto them, Ye do err, not knowing the scriptures... have ye not read that which was spoken unto you by God" (Matthew 22:29,31). As the Westminster Confession of Faith affirms:

> The supreme judge by which all controversies of religion are to be determined, and all decrees of councils, opinions of ancient writers, doctrines of men, and private spirits, are to be examined; and in whose sentence we are to rest; can be no other but the Holy Spirit speaking in the Scripture (1.10).

The same applies to controversy over Bible translation. When we approach the Word of God, we stand on hallowed ground. We must receive what God has provided for us, but we also stand on a fierce battlefield. The devil has remained relentless from the beginning in his incessant attacks upon the Word of God. In the words of Paul, we must, "Hold fast the form of sound words, which thou hast heard of me…" (2 Timothy 1:13). In the matter of Bible translation, we affirm that the Scriptures identify the text of Scripture. The biblical truths which flow from this assertion compel me to preach from the Received Text.

Robert McCurley (B.Div., Th.M. Greenville Presbyterian Theological Seminary) is an editor of The Master's Trumpet, overseeing director of Grange Press, and serves as Pastor of Greenville Presbyterian Church, Free Church of Scotland (Continuing) in Greenville, South Carolina, where he resides with his wife and five children.

15

From Certainty, to Doubt, and Back Again

Christian M. McShaffrey

When I was invited to write an essay on why I preach from the Received Text, my thoughts turned to the few times I actually tried to preach *directly* from the Greek New Testament. Those sermons were not a disaster, but only because I had essentially memorized the preaching text beforehand. Relatively few ministers reach such proficiency in the original languages that they can preach directly from the Hebrew or Greek text (i.e., sight translating from the pulpit), so most end up doing as I do each week: Preaching *from* the Greek Text *through* a translation.

This common dynamic might also account for why discussions over the authentic text are often sidetracked by debates over specific translations. This is unfortunate, but in my experience unavoidable. My contribution to this anthology, therefore, will intentionally allow the line between text and translation to remain somewhat blurred.

Ignorance Is Bliss

The sermons that first pricked my heart were preached from the Authorized Version [AV, a.k.a., *The King James Version*], so that was naturally the first version I purchased. I still own that Bible and enjoy looking back at the notes I wrote in the margin, as they memorialize the joy of a man who was hearing his Shepherd's voice for the very first time. The church I joined used a different version, but it was still based on the Received Text [TR], so the only differences I noticed were minor. One of the periodicals on the book table at church bore the snarky title "Textus Rejectus" and that was probably my first introduction to textual criticism. My Pastor always leaned toward traditional readings, so all was well at first. I had God's Word.

Certainty Somewhat Shaken

When I entered seminary, a class titled "The New Testament Text" shook my previously enjoyed certainty on two grounds. First, I had previously audited a course on Presuppositional Apologetics and was taught to bow before the epistemic lordship of Christ while studying every *loci* of the theological encyclopedia by always *assuming* the self-attesting authority of scripture and *acknowledging* that "bare evidence" does not even exist. The intellectual neutrality and evidence-based methodology of modern textual criticism seemed inconsistent with this (cf. Greg L. Bahnsen ed., *Van Til's Apologetic: Readings & Analysis*, chapters 7-9).

Second, the sheer number of disputed readings in the Greek New Testament seriously challenged my naiveté as a would-be preacher of the Word. My professor, who was himself sympathetic to traditional readings, offered the standard assurance, "None of the variants affect fundamental doctrines..." but that did not stop the scholastic clouds of doubt from rolling in over some of my favorite passages. Did Jesus really forgive an adulteress (John 7:53-8:11)? Does the Lord's Prayer end with a doxology or a reference to the devil (Matt. 6:13)? Do we really have a perfect proof-text for the Holy Trinity (1 John 5:7)? Was "God" himself manifested in the flesh (1 Timothy 3:16)? Does the Gospel of Mark actually end with no reference to the resurrection (Mark 16:9-20)?

Thus shaken, I sank myself into the study of textual criticism. The seminary library was well-stocked with books representing different sides of the issue and my crisis was soon settled as I discovered that my Puritan forefathers knew about all these textual variants, had already weighed the evidence, and came to the conclusion that God had not only *inspired* scripture, but also *preserved* it through his special care and providence (Westminster Confession of Faith, 1.8). With this conclusion, the Post-Reformation Dogmaticians also agreed (cf., Richard A. Muller, *Post-Reformation Reformed Dogmatics*, Vol. 2, 396-441).

Having embraced the historic Protestant position on the authentic text of scripture as a matter of personal conviction, my certainty returned, never to be shaken again. My interest naturally turned toward identifying the most *accurate translation* of this text, because we had begun translating Scripture in class.

The chief rule for translation assignments was to balance accuracy with readability. Another rule was "No use of thee or thou," and this led me to check my work against the New King James Version

(NKJV) rather than the AV. As I grew in my ability to translate, I came to appreciate that translation very much. I continued to use the AV in chapel speeches, but harsh criticisms from a few superiors and peers pushed me into using the NKJV more often. I regret my cowardice and capitulation. Again, the NKJV was not a poor translation. I had seen that for myself. Nevertheless, it was not as accurate as the AV, and I knew it.

The Best Translation of the Best Text

Those who sit under my ministry know that I always strive for accuracy in my teaching. This is simply part of my "precisionist" heritage, and it is also the main reason I ordinarily preach from the AV. It truly is the most *accurate* English translation of the *authentic* Greek text. Some will scoff at that claim, but even a cursory consideration of translation philosophy substantiates it. There are basically three approaches to translation: [1] Formal Equivalence translates the original on an essentially word-for-word basis, [2] Dynamic Equivalence allows the translator to "step back" and render thought-for-thought readings, and [3] Paraphrase communicates only the general idea (often with no regard to the original author's actual words). The translators of the AV employed the first model, taking as few steps away from the inspired text as necessary. The superiority of this translational philosophy can easily be demonstrated.

Word Order - The Hebrew and Greek languages are unlike English in that they enjoy great liberty when it comes to ordering words in a sentence for the sake of emphasis or euphony. Sometimes word order is significant, and sometimes it is not, but a translation committee should not make that decision for the reader. It should simply translate the text as God inspired it. Here is an innocuous example from the AV: "Then came to him the disciples of John..." (Matthew 9:14). That translation follows the *exact* word order of the original Greek. We no longer speak that way, so modern translations often "fix" the archaic sound of it by re-arranging the words: "Then the disciples of John came to him..." (ESV). Again, it is an innocuous example. No major doctrine hangs upon the word order, but the question still stands: Why rearrange words which God himself inspired? What if God *intended* to emphasize the action rather than the subject?

An example of apparent intentionality in word order is found in Jesus' evangelical exchange with Nicodemus. As a Pharisee, the man obviously had faith, but faith is only as good as its object. Jesus identifies himself as the necessary object of saving faith with a prepositional phrase that immediately follows a participle. This could be literally translated as "believing in him" or, as the AV renders it, "whosoever believeth in him" (John 3:15). The New International Version, however, relocates the preposition to the end of the sentence, seriously obfuscating the intended meaning: "that everyone who believes may have eternal life in him."

Italicized Words - While changing word order is not always necessary, adding words in the receptor language oftentimes is for the sake of readability. Whenever the AV translators did this, they italicized the words, so the reader could distinguish between that which is inspired and that which was added by editors. I will offer another innocuous example in an effort to keep the essay as irenic as possible: There is no main verb in the inspired text of Psalm 23:1. It literally reads, "The LORD my shepherd, not shall I want." It is certainly reasonable to add the assumed verb so that it reads as a complete English sentence. This is what the AV translators did: "The LORD *is* my shepherd...." Notice how the addition is indicated by italics. Again, no major doctrine is at stake there, but as a Bible reader, I want to know which words are immediately inspired by God and which words have been added by un-inspired translators. That seems like a very reasonable desire.

Thee and Thou - Critics complain that these archaisms make the AV "inaccessible" to modern man. I will admit that these words are archaic, but there is an a-historical assumption behind the complaint that must be corrected: The AV translators did not use these words because that was simply how everyone spoke in their day. They used them for the sake of translational accuracy. Both the Hebrew and Greek scriptures distinguish *singular* from *plural* personal pronouns and this cannot be done in English without using the dreaded archaisms: Thee, thou (singular) and ye, you (plural).

Thinking back to Jesus' conversation with Nicodemus, we find there a clear example of the importance of distinguishing pronouns. In John 3:3, Jesus says, "I say unto thee, Except a man be born again, he cannot see the kingdom of God." The "thee" indicates Jesus was speaking directly to Nicodemus *as an individual*. Later in the passage, however (v. 7), Jesus broadens his appeal to *all the Pharisees* (perhaps even to *the entire nation*) saying, "Ye must be born again." This shift from the singular to the plural does not appear in translations that use the word "you" for all second person personal pronouns, whether singular or plural.

Another example is found in Luke 22:31, "Simon, Simon, behold, Satan hath desired to have you, that he may sift you as wheat." The plural "you" indicates that Satan was desiring *all the apostles*. Interestingly, Jesus then shifts from the plural to the singular, *saying only to Peter*, "But I have prayed for thee, that thy faith fail not" (v. 32). Again, such nuances in the inspired text are not evident in modern versions.

Other Miscellaneous Considerations

In addition to being an accurate translation of the authentic text, the AV has many other excellent qualities which commend its continued use in the churches.

Faith - My duty as a Minister is to strengthen people's confidence in Scripture. When they sit down to read the Bible at home, I want them always to think, "This is the very Word of God." Further, members of our denomination expect Pastors to interact with the original languages as they prepare sermons. If I were to preach regularly from a modern version, I would occasionally need to correct its text or translation and that could eventually undermine people's confidence in their own copy of the scriptures. God forbid!

Intelligibility - There are archaic words in the AV, but even modern translations like the English Standard Version use words that no modern man has ever spoken in actual conversation (e.g., behold, birthstool, bitumen, lest, satraps, etc.). It is the preacher's calling *to explain* the Bible and dealing with occasional archaisms does not make that overly difficult. Sometimes, it is as simple as saying, "The word 'hitherto' means 'up to this point in time'." On a more sassy day, I might even quip, "Is it not interesting that it now takes us six words to say what used to be said with one?"

Beauty - Even unbelievers recognize the literary excellence of the AV. American writer H.L. Mencken (1880-1956) was no Christian, but he was honest enough to admit that the AV is "unquestionably the most beautiful book in the world" (*Treatise on the Gods*, 286). The outspoken atheist Richard Dawkins (b. 1941) even opined, "A native speaker of English who has never read a word of the King James Bible is verging on the barbarian" ("Why I want all our children to read the King James Bible," *The Guardian*, May 2012). The AV is *objectively* beautiful and using it in church services is one practical way to "worship the LORD in the beauty of holiness" (Psalm 29:2).

Memorability - Poetry, rhythmic prose, and sentences that contain a measure of literary cadence are much easier to memorize than colloquial speech. If you are skeptical of this claim, try an experiment: Pick a few verses from the AV and pick a brief paragraph from your local newspaper. Try to memorize both word-for-word and you will see the point proven.

Resources - Serious students of scripture will eventually desire to work directly with the inspired text. This usually starts with tools like the *Strong's Exhaustive Concordance* or a standard Greek lexicon and due to the formal equivalence of the AV, there is a more immediate correlation between its text and such tools. Even those who never delve into the original languages will find that most classic commentaries were written from and correlated with the TR and the AV.

Continuity - Fewer preachers today are using the traditional text and translation of God's Word, but in this they are parting company with some of history's favorites: Jonathan Edwards, George Whitefield, John Wesley, Charles Spurgeon, D.L. Moody, Billy Sunday, Martyn Lloyd- Jones, Billy Graham, etc. This, I admit, does not settle the matter, but it should at least curb some of the modern scorn that is expressed toward the TR and the AV.

Ecumenicity - The names listed above represent many different denominations, because the TR and the AV have been the standard text and translation in nearly every branch of Protestantism. This, in fact, is how the AV came to be. At the turn of the sixteenth century, the Puritans and the Anglicans were bitterly embroiled in controversy, and the King's decision to begin a new work of translation (the text base had already been received) brought them together. While most modern translations *claim* to be ecumenical, only the AV has been used across denominational lines for more than four centuries.

Copyright - Publishing new editions of the Greek NT and new translations has become big business in our day. I personally do not mind a good measure of free market capitalism in society, but perhaps it has come time to stop and ask the question, "Who owns the Holy Bible?" The current edition of the Received Text (Scrivener, 1894) is in the public domain and so is the Authorized Version (with a few exceptions due to royal prerogatives in the United Kingdom).

In order to obtain copyright, books must be sufficiently different from previous works and this is where modern editors and translators may face a challenge. What if the previous version was perfectly accurate in most places? How then does a publisher avoid copyright infringement and ensure profitability of the new version? I suspect that some changes are made arbitrarily. Imagine a translation committee consulting the *Thesaurus* to find synonyms for words that have already been copyrighted in previous translations. I sincerely hope that is not how it actually works, but sometimes I do wonder.

Conclusion

In this essay, I have endeavored to explain why I preach *from* the Received Text *through* the Authorized Version. My story is that of one who went from certainty, to doubt, and back again. The Good Shepherd that led me through that shadowy valley of doubt also stands ready to lead you back into the green pastures of maximal certainty. He says, "My sheep hear my voice, and I know them, and they follow me" (John 10:27). Have you?

Christian M. McShaffrey (Undergraduate studies University of St. Francis; Dipl. Worsham College of Mortuary Science; M.Div. Mid-America Reformed Seminary) serves as the Stated Clerk of the Presbytery of Wisconsin and Minnesota of the Orthodox Presbyterian Church and is the Pastor of Five Solas Church in Reedsburg, Wisconsin, where he resides with his wife and six children.

16

Why? It's the Word of God!

D. Scott Meadows

Why do I preach from the Received Text? The very wording of the question itself would tend to throw us on the defensive, and regrettably so, I believe. "Why *don't* you preach from the Received Text?" is a question we might ask opponents of the tried and true tradition of Christ's church for centuries.

A joke from my childhood comes to mind. "Why do firemen wear red suspenders?" The answer: "To hold up their pants." I would not be needlessly cheeky, but I am tempted to answer similarly. Why do I preach from the Received Text (TR)? Because it's the Word of God.

I am not unfamiliar with the controversy still raging about this issue. Voices and organizations many people find impressive advise abandoning the TR for alternatives. "New Bible" proponents print their allegedly superior texts and translations in volumes appealing to the scholars and to the masses (the former with the names of highly-credentialed academics and doctors of theology commending them, the latter with shamefully marketed target audiences).

"Resolve: The Complete New Testament" (2003) looks just like a teen fashion magazine and features the New Century Version. It is touted as having a "relevant language and format." And it sells! Scoring 4.5 stars on Amazon and #56 in the category of "Teen & Young Adult Biblical Studies." How could the Lord's work survive without it?

Admittedly, there is nothing hip or trendy about the Authorized or King James Version (AV), the premier translation for centuries of the TR in English. It is considered antiquated and archaic, like hand-crank coffee grinders and pocket watches. Modern preachers of the classic text risk instant rejection by philosophical and cultural modernists, since the underlying assumption is that newer is better, and that applies to Bible translations. Even twentieth century translations are now, in the twenty-first century, becoming passé. Multitudes seem to be members of the Bible-a-month club, and the greedy publishers love it.

I say that this is one of many reasons to preach the TR: we challenge dangerous modernity. The true biblical text is not ever-changing for each generation. It is unique, discernible, fixed, and preserved, by God's "singular care and providence kept pure in all ages," and "therefore authentical" (SLBC, 1.8). While English changes and a future revision of the AV may become warranted, at least it translates trustworthy *apographs* (copies) of the *autographs* (original manuscripts). From a long historical perspective, we are in very good company to affirm the traditional text, agreeing with people of eminent piety and scholarship.

Following guidelines for contributors to this book, I would tell you a little of my personal experience, practice, and convictions. About fifty years ago when I was nine or ten, I first started attending church in southern West Virginia—thankfully, a Bible-believing church where the Sunday school classes featured an open Bible, and the preacher read his text right from Scripture at the beginning of the sermon to expound and apply it. Not surprisingly for the time and place, the King James Version was open on every lap. I never remember struggling to understand the English found in it. Even young children in many area churches memorized countless verses from that Bible, partly motivated by little rewards we would receive for our progress. Many young people growing up today could hardly imagine such a church climate with only one Bible translation in use by just about everyone. So many of them may not even use a paper Bible primarily, but one on their smartphone. I can understand their uncertainty and confusion about Bible translations in such an environment.

When I became a man and eventually a Pastor, a plethora of translation options, most not based on the Received Text, began to appear in the pews. Admittedly, the scholarly battle within textual criticism for text superiority had been carried on for a long time, but there is typically a long delay between novelties in academia and widespread acceptance among the churches. I wasn't particularly impressed. I remember only once attempting to preach from the New American Standard Bible (NASB), and it was a most awkward experience, like shaving with another man's razor.

The local church in Exeter, New Hampshire, where I have now

pastored for thirty years had, I believe, the New King James Version (NKJV) as their pew Bibles when I arrived. I cannot recall for sure, but that may be when I began preaching from that translation. It was familiar enough to get by, and it seemed a popular choice in our circles.

Years later, the Lord brought a wonderful friend into my life—the late Mr. David Larlham from London (d. 2020). He served the Trinitarian Bible Society (TBS) for over twenty years. For much of that time, he was in a senior position as the Assistant General Secretary. His influence upon me in this matter was very helpful, along with the excellent resources of TBS for my further education—many available free on their website. Eventually, we replaced those NKJV pew Bibles with beautifully-produced AVs from TBS. I reverted to preaching from the AV without embarrassment or apology.

The more I learn, and the longer I reflect upon our practice, the more impressed I have become with the soundness of our choice to preach from the TR. In my more mature years of theological study and pastoral ministry, I have become increasingly familiar with historical theology. Paying more attention to twenty centuries of church history and the broad consensus of Christian orthodoxy, along with theological and philosophical trends spanning centuries, gives one ballast and a much better perspective to discern what is best. Generally speaking, much of what ails Christianity today is of relatively recent vintage. The pernicious influence of Rationalism and the "Enlightenment" did not leave Christian scholarship untouched. In certain respects, the Christian academy has been devastated by wicked unbelief parading as scientific objectivity, and the churches have largely followed suit.

One of the important resources I would recommend is a book by Edward F. Hills, *The King James Version Defended* (1956). Its value to me was illustrating the importance of theological and philosophical presuppositions when coming to the science of textual criticism. Reverence before God, faith in Jesus Christ, and a high view of Scripture as the Word of God are a must for drawing sound scholarly conclusions.

Since 1999, our local church has formally subscribed to the Second London Baptist Confession of Faith of 1689. In my exposition of that confession, I came to appreciate its orthodox doctrine of Scripture and the providential preservation of the Bible in the custody of Christ's church through the centuries. To quote from the confession's stated position on Scripture held in common with other Protestants,

> The Old Testament in Hebrew (which was the native language of the people of God of old), and the New Testament in Greek (which at the time of the writing of it was most generally known to the nations), being immediately inspired by God, and by His singular care and providence kept pure in all ages, are therefore authentical; so as in all controversies of religion, the church is finally to appeal to them. But because these original tongues are not known to all the people of God, who have a right unto, and interest in the Scriptures, and are commanded in the fear of God to read, and search them, therefore they are to be translated into the vulgar language of every nation unto which they come, that the Word of God dwelling plentifully in all, they may worship him in

an acceptable manner, and through patience and comfort of the Scriptures may have hope (WCF, 1.8; SLBC, 1.8).

This statement is impressive for many reasons. It was a strong and broad consensus of historic Protestant scholarship. Explicit support of it remains in the extant literature of eminent scholars like Francis Turretin and John Owen. As a product of the seventeenth century, this document was written with what came to be known as the TR consciously in view as they confessed their doctrine of Scripture in these words.

Clearly, our spiritual forefathers believed in the divine preservation through all centuries of the very words of Holy Scripture. This old, orthodox view of Scripture preservation is not as widely known and appreciated among Christians today as it should be. Francis Turretin (1623-1687), addressing the purity of the sources of the Scriptures as we now have them, asks: "Have the original texts of the Old and New Testaments come down to us pure and uncorrupted?" Speaking for Protestants, he replies: "We affirm against the papists" (*Institutes of Elenctic Theology*, 2.10). Further, John Owen (1616-1683), wrote:

> Hence, the providence of God hath manifested itself no less concerned in the preservation of the writings than of the doctrine contained in them; the writing itself being the product of his own eternal counsel for the preservation of the doctrine, after a sufficient discovery of the insufficiency of all other means for that end and purpose. And hence the malice of Satan hath raged no less against the book than

against the truth contained in it... It is true, we have not the
Αὐτόγραφα [*autographa*] of Moses and the prophets, of the
apostles and evangelists; but the ἀπόγραφα [*apographa*] or
"copies" which we have contain every iota that was in them
(*Collected Works*, Vol. 16, 300-301).

Acknowledging textual variants among ancient copies of Scripture, Owen wrote:

There is no doubt but that in the copies we now enjoy of the
Old Testament there are some diverse readings, or various
lections... But yet we affirm, that the whole Word of God, in
every letter and tittle, as given from him by inspiration, is
preserved without corruption. Where there is any variety it is
always in things of less, indeed of no, importance. God by his
providence preserving the whole entire, suffered this lesser
variety to fall out, in or among the copies we have, for the
quickening and exercising of our diligence in our search into
his Word (*Collected Works*, Vol. 16, 301).

The orthodox doctrine of Scripture preservation is vastly significant for why many of us still have confidence to preach from the
Received Text. Good books and journal articles are readily available
for the case in detail. As a working Pastor, this is not my area of
special expertise, but 1 have learned enough to continue preaching
the text of this Bible 1 hold in my hands each Sunday in church, and
daily at home. 1 habitually put on my "red suspenders" which really
need no elaborate defense except for those who are "children, tossed

to and fro, and carried about with every wind of doctrine, by the sleight of men, and cunning craftiness, whereby they lie in wait to deceive" (Ephesians 4:14).

I would not offend anyone without reason, but my convictions are settled, and I am prepared to give an account to my Lord Jesus Christ, with firm reliance upon his mercy to me. May he be pleased to use my testimony for the edification of all who read it. Amen.

D. Scott Meadows (B.S.E.E. West Virginia Institute of Technology; M.A. Atlantic Baptist Bible College), author, editor, conference speaker, and Pastor of Calvary Baptist Church of Exeter, New Hampshire, where he resides with his wife.

17

The Christian Bible
Can Be Trusted

Pooyan Mehrshahi

"The Christian Bible cannot be trusted, because people have distorted and falsified [*tahrif*] the original words of the Torah [Old Testament] and the *Enjil* [Gospels or the New Testament]." As a young boy, living in Iran, I heard this argument from my teachers in the Madrasah [Islamic school], when the subject of the Holy Scriptures would come up. "The Christians and the Jews have changed their Scriptures," was the usual pronouncement. Therefore, having been brought up under such indoctrination in the Islamic Republic of Iran, I was filled with prejudice and self-righteousness, which made me dismiss the Bible as being the authentic, reliable, and pure revelation of God. However, later in life, by the grace of God, I was brought under conviction of sin, was brought to a saving knowledge of the Lord Jesus Christ, and gained a trust in the inspiration and preservation of the text of the Holy Scriptures.

My study and transition to a Biblical conviction on the confessional view of the doctrine of providential preservation was mainly encouraged by my gospel outreach among the Russelites (more commonly known as Jehovah's Witnesses) and the Muslims. These encounters made me study the underlying text of the Old and New Testaments.

For many years now, I have used Received Text Bibles (in English, the Authorized or King James Version) in my ministry and outreach, and have found that it has strengthened and helped my endeavors to reach Muslims and other unconverted people. I have found that having a standard, textually stable, theologically faithful, accurate Bible is necessary in a faithful pulpit and evangelism ministry. I will aim to explain my reasons in an untechnical format, with a slant on ministry to the multicultural and increasingly Islamic and pagan society in the West.

The following subject headings are attacked by the critics of the Gospel, including many Islamic apologists and unbelieving textual critics in their online and printed publications. From personal encounters, I find that the tech-savy and informed Muslim apologists are using the critical teaching of the Reformed and evangelical authors and internet debaters and teachers as ammunition against the gospel and the authenticity and infallibility of the Holy Scriptures. On a side note: To my surprise, some years ago, I discovered that the center for the training of Iranian Islamic clerics in the city of Qom, are publishing translations of textual critics of our day, who are popular among evangelical and Reformed teachers and institutions. The ammunition to attack the infallibility of the Word of God is fueled by these evangelicals who are being quoted by the enemies of the gospel. This highlights the need to return to a theologically robust and presuppositional understanding of the doctrine of Scripture and its divine preservation. The following are a few points which I find needful in an effective ministry and outreach:

A Standard Text

The Bibles based on the Received Text [TR] have, since the Reformation period, been the standard and generally accepted Christian scriptures. This can be seen in many of the historic translations (e.g. Luther's German Version, the Authorized Version in English, the Van Dyke Version in Arabic, the Statenvertaling Version in Dutch, the 1856 Persian Version, and many others). This fact is well known by educated Muslim apologists, who argue that the Christian Church does not have one standard Bible. The sidelining of the historic TR Bibles and a pursuit of ever increasing modern translations have fueled their false arguments. In the English language, the Authorized Version has been the uniting text among the churches and respected as that throughout the world. The informed unbelieving critics often say that the church does not know which Bible to use. To this day, the AV and similar historic translations in other languages remain the common Bible used in Africa, India, the Far East, the Middle East, the West Indies, and by many in the Western world. The TR-based historic translations give the church a standard and unifying text of the Holy Scriptures.

A Stable Text

The translations based on the TR, by their very nature, are not constantly changing according to any supposed new textual discoveries and evolution of textual critical thought and theories. What a comfort to the church, especially in her endeavors to spread the good news of the glorious message of this holy Word of God and the salvation that is found therein. She can rely on the words in her hand, that it comes from God and has been faithfully preserved and translated and tested for centuries by believers all over the world.

In contrast, the critical explanations contained in the footnotes of many Bibles, including the New King James Version, actually undermine the unchanging nature of the text of Scripture to the common reader. The common man reads the footnotes which often begin with the words "This is not contained in the oldest and best manuscripts." What is the average reader to think? This suggests that the words contained in this Bible may not be the true text, and yet they are contained on this page of this Bible! The last twelve verses of Mark's Gospel and the woman caught in adultery passages come to mind. What might be helpful to the scholar and seminary student will not be helpful to those who are reading the scriptures for the first time, or simply for their daily spiritual nourishment. How can we put our trust in a Bible which questions the authenticity of certain verses within its own pages? Further, how can the underlying manuscripts also be trusted if they differ from one another in so many places? Is the ordinary reader, with his limited knowledge, really supposed to decide a reading? The footnotes offered by the "experts" betray that they themselves are not even sure.

A stable text can be relied upon, read, studied, meditated upon and memorized for edification, preaching, and evangelism. The Psalmist says, "Thy word have I hid in mine heart, that I might not sin against thee" (Psalm 119:11). How can an ever-changing text of Scripture be retained in the heart and mind? It cannot be memorized. An ever-changing text does not help remedy the many spiritual problems in churches and in the ministry that Christ has commissioned.

A Theologically Faithful Text

Even though many who claim to know and promote a critical view of the text of Scripture, say that no doctrine is affected in the critical text, yet this is not a strong footing for someone who claims to believe in the doctrine of the preservation of Scripture, as stated in the Second London Baptist Confession of Faith 1.8. Many of the textual variants and omissions in the critical text are theologically significant, rather than mere grammatical variations, such as an "and" or "is." It is true that one can defend the deity of Christ from a critical text translation, including even the Watchtower's New World Translation, yet why use a theologically weak text when the TR offers a theologically robust, complete, and faithful text of the revealed Word? TR-based translations do not undermine, but uphold fundamental doctrines like the virgin birth, the deity of Christ, the Holy Trinity, and the fulfillment of prophecy.

The theological instability of the critical text is very much attacked by the Islamic apologists and publishing houses, who quote textual critics, such as Bruce Metzger and Bart Ehrman and popularizers such as F.F. Bruce and other more modern proponents of the critical text. The following words from Daniel B. Wallace are a classic example:

We do not have now—in our critical Greek texts or any translations thereof—exactly what the authors of the New Testament wrote. Even if we did, we would not know it. There are many, many places in which the text of the New Testament is uncertain (Hixson and Gurry, eds., *Myths & Mistakes in New Testament Textual Criticism*, xii).

The theological weakness of the critical text Bibles undermines gospel outreach, as we need all the faithful revelation of God, as he has revealed, not less. When the cults or informed Muslims challenge me on the deity of Christ, l happily quote from 1 Timothy 3:16 or 1 John 5:7. Yet in my experience they immediately ask for a modern Bible, or say that evangelical textual critics deny the validity of these texts, and l therefore ought not defend the deity of Christ and the doctrine of the Holy Trinity from these texts. These are the example texts that are modified or deleted from the critical text translations: 1 Timothy 3:16 "God was manifest in the flesh" and 1 John 5:7 "For there are three that bear record in heaven, the Father, the Word, and the Holy Ghost: and these three are one."

Our Reformed confessions of faith and the theological writings of the Reformers, the Puritans and the theologians, as well as many sermons of bygone preachers, have defended the fundamental doctrines of the Christian faith by referring to those passages that are missing or weakened in the critical text translations. The question should be asked: How can one hold to these confessions and deny the proof texts that are part of these Reformed Standards? Or, is it not amazing that the Lord has blessed sermons and writings of many preachers, who based their sermons on texts that are now deemed as not part of the inspired text of scriptures? One cannot imagine the Lord putting his stamp of approval and benediction on verses that supposedly are not inspired, but rather scribal mistakes or editorial additions.

In my opinion, someone who holds consistently to the Reformed confessions of faith must also be consistent in their upholding of the doctrine of the preservation of Scripture as taught in them (cf., Westminster Confessions of Faith and 1689 Baptist Confession of Faith, 1.8).

A Correct Textual Family and Translation Method

The Received Text is mainly based on the vast majority of extant readings. It is the fullest and most authentic text, which has been preserved by God and used by the true people of God. The critical text is generally based on the minority of available texts, which differ at significant points with the TR. Because of the discrepancies, the critical-text translations insert many suggestive or speculative footnotes which can unsettle a normal reader of the New Testament regarding the authenticity of the inspired Word of God. The unstable textual basis of the critical text is described and warned against in Proverbs 24:21, "My son, fear thou the LORD ... and meddle not with them that are given to change." The phrase "given to change" means "changers."

How can one defend the authority and authenticity of every text of Scripture, if one is never certain whether the next printed edition of the critical text may include some new readings or omit some which were previously deemed inspired words? Our Lord said, "Man shall not live by bread alone, but by every word that proceedeth out of the mouth of God" (Matthew 4:4). Every man, both young and old, is a living soul that needs every word that proceeds out of the mouth of God: not most of it, not ninety percent of it, but a hundred percent of it, which God has promised to preserve for his people down through the ages. Every word then must be faithfully translated as accurately and as literally as possible.

Conclusion

There have been certain times in general outreach work in our community that we hear criticism of the use of the Authorized Version, mainly due to its seeming archaic and supposedly difficult "Elizabethan" language. Without fail, the criticism has come from those who profess to be Christians, who are educated and have English as their mother tongue! I have not heard any criticism of the text of Scripture from people of other cultures, except those who have read the critical statements of the modern "Christian" textual critics and Muslim apologists.

Yes, I admit that a translation such as the Authorized Version and similar translations in other languages require some getting used to, and learning certain new words and expressions. This is true of any field of study. When we study any secular subject, no one questions the fact that there are many new technical words and expressions that need to be learned. Why should we not expect the same when studying the revealed will of God from heaven? This is also applicable to any modern or older translations in any language. There are a significant number of words in all modern critical text translations that are not readily used or understood by the modern reader. Therefore the arguments on relevance and archaism cannot be accepted as valid or weighty. The reader of the Word of God cannot be expected to be an inattentive and unteachable reader.

In 1999, the Lord, by his grace, brought me to a saving knowledge of the Lord Jesus Christ. As a young man coming from a different culture, living in a multicultural society, what kind of Bible did I look for? I was searching for a Bible that was relevant to me. I was not concerned that the Bible was difficult to read, or that I would have to use my dictionary or to re-read certain passages. I desired a Bible which was the most accurate, most stable, textually-faithful and complete translation of the inspired Hebrew and Greek texts. I knew from James 1:8 that, "A double minded man is unstable in all his ways." Can this not also be applied to a Bible that is based on an unstable text?

My pulpit ministry, pastoral counseling, open-air outreach, and personal evangelism among English speakers, as well as among the many hundreds and thousands of Iranian and Afghan Muslims, is more effective due to a consistent use of and confidence in the Word of God as preserved in the Received Text, and in translations that are founded on it.

In this essay, I have sought simply to highlight some basic points defending the Received Text, preserved to this day, as the authentic and kept Word of God. This Sword of the Spirit was forged and maintained by the power of God, and it will be used by him, and by his true church, till the end. The words of John Bunyan's character, Mr. Great-heart in reference to Mr. Valiant's sword is appropriate in contrasting the Received Text Bibles against their critical text counterparts:

GREAT-HEART: "Then said Great-heart to Mr. Valiant-for-truth, Thou hast worthily behaved thyself. Let me see thy sword. So he showed it him. When he had taken it in his hand, and looked thereon a while, he said, 'Ha! it is a right Jerusalem blade' (Isaiah 2:3)."

VALIANT: "It is so. Let a man have one of these blades, with a hand to wield it and skill to use it, and he may venture upon an angel with it. He need not fear its holding, if he can but tell how to lay on. Its edges will never blunt. It will cut flesh and bones, and soul and spirit, and all' (Ephesians 6:12-17; Hebrews 4:12)" (*Pilgrim's Progress*, Part 2).

Pooyan Mehrshahi (B.Sc. Computer Science, Dipl. Pastoral Theology White-field College of the Bible, Northern Ireland) is chairman of Parsa Trust (an Iranian Reformed ministry), leading the Persian Bible translation project with the Trinitarian Bible Society, a lecturer and trustee at Salisbury Reformed Seminary, and Pastor of Providence Baptist Chapel, Cheltenham, UK, where he resides with his wife Becky and four children.

18

My Journey to the Received Text

Mark L. R. Mullins

I became a Christian in 1984 as a university student at a mission run by Durham Christian Union. After the meeting, I was taken back to the house of an Anglican ordinand who was studying theology, and he explained the gospel to me from Ephesians chapter 2. I had never heard before that it was by grace we are saved through faith and that not of ourselves, but the gift of God (Ephesians 2:8-9). My eyes were opened for the first time to the truth that Christ had paid for my sins and I have always marked that day, February 14, 1984 as the day I was born again. I remember the following Saturday lying on my bed reading the first chapter of John's Gospel and being amazed that I could understand it for the first time.

I mention this because my introduction to Christ went hand-in-hand with my introduction to the New International Version of the

Bible (NIV). It was a version in modern English unlike the versions I had used when I was growing up, so it was easy to believe that my understanding of the Bible was connected to the easy-to-understand English of that translation. The barriers to understanding the Bible which were raised by older versions like the King James Bible had been removed. For the first ten years of my life as a Christian I was taken in by this assumption, while at the same time feeling that there was something missing in the NIV, something which made it feel somewhat anemic. The version did not seem to plumb the depths of God's greatness and his majesty, but for years I continued to use it, because I knew no differently.

In 1992, I began participating in an organization called *Intercessors For Britain* that prayed for the nation. It was a more conservative organization than the very charismatic church I was attending at the time, and it was the first time that I heard arguments voiced against the NIV. They recommended using the New American Standard Bible (NASB), because they said it was more accurate than the NIV. The issue of the Received Text was not addressed and, at that time I was unaware it was an issue, so I began to use the NASB. After about two years, however, I found this version did not flow well, and as an Englishman, I was uneasy with the American spellings.

Up until that time I had been put off by the King James Version, because I had been attending the well-known Anglican charismatic church, Holy Trinity Brompton, where the controversial *Alpha Course* began. When it came to Bible versions, Nicky Gumbel, the person running the course, was rather dismissive of the King James Version. He would cite, with some ridicule, the passage where Saul covered his feet (1 Samuel 24:3) to demonstrate that this was an arcane translation that was unable to communicate straightforward concepts, such as obeying the call of nature. I had therefore come to assume that the King James Version was out of date and irrelevant.

By August 1994, however, I had grown dissatisfied with all the modern versions. The New King James was being recommended to me as a good translation, so it gave me cause to ask myself, "Well, why not try the King James Version itself?" After all, it had stood the test of time, and I knew, despite the criticisms made in the *Alpha Course*, that it was written in beautiful prose and had a reverence that was not present in modern versions. At that time I came across a book called *New Age Versions* by Gail Riplinger, which advocated strongly for the King James Version. In retrospect, I regard this book as extreme and recognize that many statements in it are inaccurate. This is well documented in the online article by David Cloud, "The Problem With *New Age Bible Versions*" (*O Timothy Magazine*, Vol. 11, Issue 8, 1994; accessible at wayoflife.org).

Once I began to read the King James Version I never looked back and felt in a real sense that I had come home. This was my journey to the King James Version. For a number of years I was content to remain in a position where I used the King James Version, because I regarded it as the best version but did not contend for it. That changed in the summer of 2016.

In the month of July, I visited a small fundamentalist Baptist Church in the West Country where the Pastor spoke of the King James Version of the Bible as the inspired Word of God in English. A few days later, I attended another church for a wedding, where I saw a Pastor generously present a Bible to the bride and groom at the end of the service. This seemed like an excellent present, because it would point the bride and groom to the only sure foundation for a successful marriage, namely God's Word, which is a lamp unto our feet and a light unto our path (Psalm 119:105). I discovered later, however, that the Bible presented to the couple was *The Message* by Eugene Peterson, which is a paraphrase that seeks to convey the author's understanding of the scriptures in today's language. I do not believe that *The Message* can properly be described as the Bible.

That August, I was asked to speak at my old church. It was a traditional Pentecostal church that had rejected the modern ways which had so corrupted the movement. A week before the event, while prayerfully considering the message I should bring, I determined to speak on "Bible Versions." This is a topic I had previously not addressed. There was a lot of work to be done, but I was greatly assisted in this task by Malcolm Watts' excellent booklet, *The Lord Gave The Word*. This booklet greatly impacted my thinking and led me to attend the Salisbury Conference where I met various Reformed ministers. This was to be the beginning of my journey to accept the doctrines of grace and Reformed theology. Also, very helpful during this time was Dr. Edward F. Hills' book *The King James Version Defended.*

My research led me to an examination of the manuscripts that made up the Old and New Testaments, and the doctrine of the providential preservation of scripture. This was a new way of looking at things, but it made complete sense. The Bible claims to be the pure and inspired Word of God. We find this throughout the scriptures. Psalm 12:6-7 reads, "The words of the LORD are pure words: as silver tried in a furnace of earth, purified seven times. Thou shalt keep them, O LORD, thou shalt preserve them from this generation for ever." These words will stand forever (Isaiah 40:8). The Lord Jesus said that his words will never pass away (Matthew 24:35). Paul says, "All scripture is given by inspiration of God, and is profitable for doctrine, for reproof, for correction, for instruction in righteousness" (2 Timothy 3:16). Peter writes, "Being born again not of corruptible seed, but of incorruptible, by the word of God which liveth and abideth forever" (1 Peter 1:23-25). All these scriptures speak of the preservation of the Lord's Word forever. That Word was given in the Hebrew Old Testament and the Greek New Testament. I am fully convinced we must maintain, by faith, that the scriptures have been kept pure throughout the generations, which is why I hold to the Received Text.

I mentioned earlier that I went to a church in the West Country where the Pastor taught that the King James Version is the inspired English translation and is as much the Word of God as the original manuscripts, because the Holy Spirit inspired the translators in the same way he inspired the original writers of scripture. I came to understand, however, that this not only goes too far, but is in fact heretical. After giving the series of talks at my old church, I wrote to this Pastor and arranged to meet him in the spring of 2017 in a hospital where I was visiting someone. While I was waiting, I saw a Mormon enter carrying his *Book of Mormon*. I realized that this Pastor had fallen into the same error as the Mormons, albeit in a less obvious way. If we believe that the translators could have been inspired in the same way as the original authors, then why can't God speak again and keep the canon of scripture open? The Bible is immediately inspired in the original Hebrew and Greek, however, not in translations. With that distinction firmly in place, we can also trust the accuracy and authority of the King James Version.

Mark L.R. Mullins (B.A. in Economics, University of Durham; Diploma in Law, University of Westminster) practices as a criminal barrister in London and is the minister of Strangers Rest Evangelical Church, a Reformed Church in Shadwell, East London. Mark is also a trustee of Christian Watch and on the Council of the Protestant Alliance.

19

The Invincible Word

Christopher Myers

Jesus said, "For verily I say unto you, Till heaven and earth pass, one jot or one tittle shall in no wise pass from the law, till all be fulfilled" (Matthew 5:18). It is one thing to listen to what people say about the Word of God, but it is an entirely different thing to see what Scripture teaches concerning itself. This verse affirms that God's Word is immutable or unchangeable. Further, that attribute is here applied to every letter, every syllable, every word, and every sentence. Because this is true, it will conquer, it will prevail, like light against darkness. The Word of God is invincible.

The word 'verily' invites us to pay closer attention. The Lord Jesus did not come to destroy the law, but rather to fulfil it. Due to its very nature, Scripture cannot be destroyed. Let us consider, in detail, how Christ explains this.

Jesus says, "Till heaven and earth pass, one jot or one tittle shall in no wise pass from the law." He meant by 'heaven and earth' all things. Look around you and behold the sky, the stars, the universe, the grass, the city, the people, even heaven and earth will pass one day. The day is coming when they will be rolled up like a scroll, and every man will appear before the judgment seat of Jesus Christ to receive each according to his works. Notice, however, that until that day arrives, heaven and earth stand indestructible.

There is, for example, no climate change that is great enough to end the world before the appointment of our Lord Jesus. We should be good stewards of the creation until the new heavens and the new earth arrive. Nonetheless, the present heavens and earth will continue until that appointed day. As we look and wait for that day, we can rest assured that the Bible also will never pass away.

When we say "The Bible" we are referring to the *written* word, because this is specifically what Jesus declared to be indestructible. While many see the written word as foolishness, it is the primary means of grace through which men are saved. The Bible announces wrath to come, hellfire and brimstone, and eternal torments upon the unrighteous. This is true, because the Lord has spoken it. These truths abide that all men may receive the message to flee from the wrath to come. It is only through this Word that salvation may be known, and it is only when the last person is saved that heaven and earth will finally pass away.

The Bible abides, and it is also unchangeable (even to its minutest detail). The Holy Spirit, speaking through Jesus Christ, affirmed this attribute before the scholars of his day. Until heaven and earth pass, neither one jot (likely referencing the smallest Hebrew consonant) nor one tittle (likely referencing the smallest Hebrew vowel point) shall be lost. The obvious lesson is this: Even that which may seem insignificant in Scripture will be preserved by God.

Understanding this is crucial because if we do not possess God's Word, we cannot confidently preach God's Word, and people will not be converted. Essential to effective preaching is affirming the authority of God's Word. We cannot preach with full certainty if we think the Bible has been corrupted and must rely on man's words to clarify it. Where is the power of God's Word if we cast doubt upon it? How will that convert souls? How can the preacher point definitively to the Word of God and proclaim, "Thus saith the LORD God"? Furthermore, how can we translate with any certainty if we do not have every jot and tittle?

A historic assault has been launched against God's Word which denies that every jot and tittle has been preserved. Scholars say they can prove that Scripture has been corrupted by pointing to all the variant readings that exist. They say that since there are so many thousands of variants, the Bible must not have been preserved. This, however, is not a battle against flesh and blood (or manuscripts and versions).

There has always been a synagogue of Satan and a synagogue of Christ, a Bible of Satan and a Bible of Christ. This can be traced throughout Scripture. Why, for example, did Paul write, "Ye see how large a letter 1 have written unto you with mine own hand" (Galatians 6:11)? He wrote this because there were apparently false teachers on the scene who were writing and circulating counterfeit scriptures. There have always been false prophets. The Apostle John also dealt with some (i.e., Gnostics) that believed they had "the secret" Word of God, but they had false scriptures, which have always been in competition with the one true Word of God.

Satan set up his own competing Bible that the true Word of God might be hampered, but he was not successful. This is evident in the writings of the church fathers, when they testify to the necessity of accepting the true Word of God and rejecting others. Not all of these early theologians did this faithfully. Origen, for example, accepted other scriptures, but as time went on, the Lord Jesus made sure that his one true Bible, written in the Hebrew and Greek, was preserved, and thus vindicated as invincible.

So victorious was the Word that Satan had to try a different tactic. He caused many to stop reading their Bibles altogether, especially in the Medieval era. During that era, people looked to the words of men more than they did the Word of God, because the Bible had become inaccessible. It was available only in Latin, and in that translation there were corruptions. This was very convenient for the kingdom of darkness, because those corruptions led to new doctrines. Where, for example, do you find justification for things like purgatory? These things came from man's traditions, being based on apocryphal writings, and were thrust upon the church as God's Word. This came about because men started declaring themselves as a god in the church, ruling in the stead of Christ.

After the Middle Ages, the Turks arose and the Ottoman empire conquered Constantinople in AD 1453. This capital city of the Greek-speaking Eastern church had faithfully kept countless copies of the Greek New Testament. Some men escaped the Turks and fled with these copies to Italy, Spain, and North Africa. In God's good providence, this led to a renewed interest amongst scholars in going back to the sources (i.e., humanism). They discovered differences in the Latin versions from the original Greek texts. This led to a desire to collate the Greek texts and to compare what had been received in the churches with what they had been reading in the Latin. The Pope was not happy with this.

There now appeared to be two Bibles: (1) Satan's Bible with gnostic heretics writing false scriptures and twisting the true scriptures, and (2) the received and preserved Word of God. Which one was authentic? The Pope said it was the Latin one, but the Protestants, the Bible-believers, disagreed. The true Word of God had been received in the churches, passed down through all ages of the church, and preserved with every jot and tittle. These two different Bibles were then translated into English. The first, the English Douay-Rheims Version was translated from the Latin Vulgate, and the English King James Version (KJV) was translated from the Received Hebrew and Greek text, preserving every jot and tittle of the Word of God. The KJV was published in 1611 and continues a faithful translation even today, over four hundred years later. Even then, however, the battle did not end.

In the late nineteenth century, there were scholars, Brooke Foss Westcott and Fenton John Anthony Hort, who found some ancient manuscripts in Egypt and thought these proved that the Received Text contained verses that could not have been words of the Apostles and Prophets. They were working under the presupposition that since the older manuscripts were closer to the age of the apostles, they must be closer to what the Bible originally looked like. These men were not orthodox in theology, but some began to embrace in their scholarship. Men of God, such as B. B. Warfield, Charles Hodge, and A. A. Hodge had already become sympathetic to evolutionary methodology for understanding creation and history, so why not apply this kind of thinking to the text as well?

Earlier efforts in this same kind of naturalistic thinking, would include men like Brian Walton (1600-1661). He was an Anglican Bishop who compiled textual variants under naturalistic presuppositions and many of the Reformed orthodox, like John Owen and Francis Turretin, wrote against his theories because his view of the Bible was practically atheistic.

Afterward, there arose a Jesuit priest, Richard Simon, who took Walton's theory to what he believed was its logical end: We need an authority higher than naturalistic methodologies to identify the authentic text of scripture. To Simon, this authority was the Pope of Rome.

By the 1870s, atheists and heretics were taking the actual theory of evolution and applying it to the Bible. They ended up agreeing with Simon and Walton, whom the Reformed orthodox had previously opposed. Thus developed modern textual criticism, resulting in an "eclectic text" of the Bible that ordinarily prefers the oldest manuscripts available, regardless of whether they are trustworthy. The text of these "oldest manuscripts" were not those received and used by orthodox churches.

There are two main codices, *Sinaiticus* and *Vaticanus*, which modern textual critics regard as supremely trustworthy. However, Sinaiticus had uninspired writings attached to it. Vaticanus contained the Apocrypha and its provenance was unknown before coming into the possession of the Vatican by AD 1475. The Protestant churches knew about Vaticanus and had rejected it due to its corruptions. Once again, we see Satan setting up his own Bible against the true one. This battle continues.

You still have two Bibles today. You have versions that are based on the evolutionary methods of reconstructing the Hebrew and Greek, and which have the stamp of approval from the Pope of Rome and all those who embrace an evolutionary methodology. On the other hand, you have versions based on methods which assume providential preservation, as professed at the time of the Protestant Reformation. Which Bible should you use? I offer this essay in hope that you will embrace the Word of God that has been preserved with every jot and tittle through every age.

Do you see the different starting points? To understand the Bible you must start with the Bible, not with the new evolutionary method of modern textual criticism. The modern method treats the Bible like any other piece of literature. I am here sounding the alarm because there is a movement amongst the scholars of this world that will result in another major change of the text of scripture. It is called the CBGM [Coherence-based Genealogical Method]. It consists in taking a computer algorithm and applying values to the different manuscripts in order to come up with a new Greek text. The changes will be seen in the Nestle-Aland and United Bible Societies Greek New Testaments, but the work is not projected to be completed until 2030.

To my knowledge, there is not a Ph.D. credentialed textual critic alive today who affirms the providential preservation of the Word of God as defined by the Reformed orthodox. Many godly men who follow these scholars may personally hold to the doctrine of providential preservation, but this is inconsistent. This is why the consistent scholars do not hold to it. For example, this is why Daniel Wallace says that providential preservation was an invention of the Reformation. Beware of academic scholars who deny that the Word of God is invincible.

The words of Jesus Christ were literally true. Every jot and tittle is preserved and always will be, for this is the very nature of the Bible. It does not need to be reconstructed. We have the true Bible.

Modern translations based on Satan's Bible, that omit some of the Word of God, include the New American Standard Bible, New International Version, English Standard Version, and many others. Other modern versions that utilize the Received Text, especially of the Greek New Testament, include the New King James Version, Modern King James Version, Modern English Version, and the Jubilee Bible. Sadly, some textual and translation errors have been identified in such versions. Because of this, they have never replaced the most trusted English translation: The Authorised Version, which has stood the test of time. Since the standardization of spelling and the correcting of some printing errors in 1769, there has never been a demonstrable error in translation identified.

This version is the Bible of the English Protestant Reformation, demonstrated by the fact that it is the foundation of the Westminster Confession of Faith and Catechisms. It is also the Bible of genuine revival, as faithful preaching of it resulted in the Great Awakening and subsequent revivals. It is the Bible of missions, as was proven in the great efforts of the nineteenth century. It is the Bible that changed the English-speaking world, its literature, vocabulary, and ways of thinking. It is the Bible that continues to this day to be the most read and trusted by Bible-believing Christians.

Christopher Myers (B.S. James Madison University; M.Div. Liberty Theological Seminary) is the Pastor of Phoenix Reformed Presbyterian Church (Reformed Presbyterian Church of North America) and resides in Glendale, Arizona, with his wife and four children.

20

Train Up a Child

Jeffrey T. Riddle

Why do I preach from the Received Text? As anyone can witness from reading the articles in this collection, there are many approaches that one might take to answering this question. I am going to take a somewhat more autobiographical approach.

I was born in 1965. In the small rural Baptist church of my childhood in the Lowcountry of South Carolina, there were not multiple translations of the Bible available for use in the pew. When the Pastor stood in the pulpit to preach and asked the congregation to turn to his text, the whisking of thin leaves could be heard, turning from page to page, till we found the book, chapter, and verse. Some had smaller printed Bibles and some larger. Some of those Bibles had expensive leather covers, while others were cheap, mass-produced paperbacks, like the ones given to the children ferried to the church by our bus ministry. When all the hearers reached the appointed passage, however, there was unity in that each was reading from the same translation, the King James Version (KJV). At the time, I did not realize the importance of this translation as a cultural monument of the English language, nor did I know that part of its significance rested in the fact that it was a translation based on the traditional Protestant printed editions of the original Hebrew and Greek texts. I probably did not know there were other Bible translations.

On the bookshelf of my study, I still have a copy of my childhood Bible, a small black leather Cambridge edition of the Holy Bible in the King James translation given to me by my parents on Christmas Day, December 25, 1973. I can still read the Epistle Dedicatory in that volume in which the translators note that the king "out of deep judgement" had commissioned the translators "out of the Sacred Tongues" to set forth "one more exact Translation of the holy Scriptures into the *English Tongue*." I also have on my shelf a green covered edition of the *Living Bible: Paraphrased*. It was also given to me by my parents, four years later, on Christmas Day, December 25, 1977. I did not realize at the time that this second Bible represented the inroads of modern texts, translations, and paraphrases of the Bible, reaching even into our remote little church. These new Bibles would eventually rival and attempt to undermine not only the preeminent standing and use of the King James Version but, most importantly, the traditional text upon which it was based.

I also find it interesting, as I look now at those two volumes on my desk, to note that the little KJV is in much worse shape than the *Living Bible*. The faded leather cover is filled with various nicks and scratches. Most of the original black reference tabs have been worn away, though a few remain. The edges of the pages are yellowed, and some are torn from constant fingering and turning. In occasional places verses are underlined in pen, though this is rare, since I was taught as a child that one mark of reverence for the Bible was that one should not overly write on its pages. Another sign of reverence I was taught in my home was that the Bible was always to be placed on the uppermost shelf of the bookcase, and no other books were ever to be placed above, over, or on it. In contrast, my copy of the *Living Bible* is in much better shape. The cover has some marks from wear, but the interior pages are still rather crisp, even after all these years, and I could not find a single verse underlined within it, nor do I ever remember memorizing a single verse from it. My parents likely gave me this second book thinking I might find it easier to comprehend, but I apparently found very little practical use for it. Maybe that was a sign of things to come.

In my first semester of college, I took an Introduction to the New Testament class and had my initial encounter with the modern historical critical method. A required textbook for this class was an inexpensive copy of the Revised Standard Version (RSV, 1980 edition). This was the first modern translation of which I made serious use. I also later picked up the hardcover *Oxford Annotated Bible with the Apocrypha* in the RSV, edited by Herbert G. May and Bruce M. Metzger. I used both of these Bibles during my seminary days at the flagship institution of my evangelical denomination. In 1990, just before leaving for two years of service as a short-term missionary in post-communist Budapest, Hungary, my in-laws gave me a sleek thinline copy of the *New International Version* (1984 edition). As I studied and learned Hungarian, I took notice that many of the

Magyar believers still used the classic Protestant *Károli Gáspár* translation of 1590, even as a modern revision of it, conforming to the modern critical text, was produced on its four hundredth anniversary in 1990.

When I returned to the United States, I took a call to serve as Pastor at a small rural congregation in Virginia and began preaching from my thinline NIV. After all, I heard that it had supposedly become the most popular English translation among American evangelicals. After a few years I began taking courses at a nearby mainline Protestant denomination seminary and eventually completed a doctoral dissertation there in New Testament. I did not agree with the school's theological perspective, but it was accredited, and this was in the pre-internet days when all classes had to be done in-person. At the time, the school required that the *New Revised Standard Version* (1989) be used for all academic projects.

As a Pastor, I became convinced that the greatest need of the people I served was to build up their knowledge of the scriptures. I also found that I was not creative enough to produce an endless series of unique topical sermons. I thus made a commitment to verse-by-verse expositional preaching and began working my way through books of the Bible. The first book I tackled was James. I had used this book in discipleship in Hungary, suggesting that new believers read and meditate on one chapter each day, so that the whole five-chapter book could be digested Monday-Friday. Then, after Lord's Day worship, the process could be repeated, till the book was thoroughly mastered.

As a student I had been warned against *eisegesis*, reading meaning into the text, as opposed to *exegesis*, drawing meaning out of the text. This insight helped spur me on to more extensive study of the text in the original languages. At some point I picked up a copy of the Trinitarian Bible Society's edition of the Bible which bound the Bomberg/Ginsburg Hebrew Old Testament and the Greek *Textus Receptus* together into one volume. As I began to prepare more carefully for preaching, comparing the traditional and modern critical texts, I encountered differences between them and the translations made from them.

With regard to text, I began to notice the "missing verses." This included not only the "big passages" (the ending of Mark, Mark 16:9-20, and the account of the woman taken in adultery, John 7:53-8:11), but many, many other smaller differences of a word, phrase, or verse throughout the Bible. In a seminary class, I had written a paper on the doxology of the Lord's Prayer (Matthew 6:13b), in which I had defended the originality and authenticity of this text as the fitting ending to the model prayer. As I preached through the Sermon on the Mount as a Pastor, I became even more convinced this was the case.

With regard to translation, I began to notice the many incidences of dynamic equivalence in the NIV. I well remember one of these. I was preaching through Christ's teaching on the final resurrection in John 5:28-29. The NIV reads:

Do not be amazed at this, for a time is coming when all who are in their graves will hear his voice and come out—those that have done good will rise to live, and those who have done evil will rise to be condemned.

It was that final phrase in v. 29 that chiefly caught my attention: "those that have done good will rise to live, and those who have done evil will rise to be condemned." When I looked at the Greek text, I saw that the NIV failed to capture a most vivid parallel that stood in the original Greek (as it reads in both the TR and the modern critical text; underline added): οι τα αγαθα ποιησαντες εις αναστασιν ζωης οι δε τα φαυλα πραξαντες εις αναστασιν κρισεως. The underlined words reveal two parallel prepositional phrases which could be literally translated as "into the resurrection of life" and "into the resurrection of condemnation." The NIV, however, renders the two prepositional phrases in the original text as future tense verbs modified by an infinitive: "will rise to live" and "will rise to be condemned." This kind of "dynamic" translation is very common in the NIV.

I then looked at the King James Version and noted its superior formal equivalence rendering: "they that have done good, unto the resurrection of life; and they that have done evil, unto the resurrection of damnation" (v. 29b). It not only dawned on me that the KJV was a better translation of the Greek original on a linguistic level, but also on a theological level in that it brought out into the open Christ's central teaching on a twofold final "resurrection" of the just and of the unjust. Disappointingly, in the NIV's rendering of v. 29, the word "resurrection" made no explicit appearance at all.

Issues related to both text and translation continued to arise as I attempted rightly to divide the scriptures. After much thought, prayer, study, and teaching, I determined that my restless conscience would not have peace till I came to some clear conclusions on my doctrine of Scripture. If the preaching of the Word was to be at the center of my ministry, I had to have confidence and certainty as to what the Word of God is. I gladly embraced the traditional Protestant original language texts of the Christian Bible: the Masoretic text of the Hebrew Old Testament and the *Textus Receptus* of the Greek New Testament. I began teaching on the topic of textual criticism and offering a defense of the authenticity of passages like the traditional ending of Mark (which I described as a "slam dunk" for the traditional text). I also made the decision to abandon the NIV. At first, I moved to the New King James Version (NKJV) and even wrote a long position paper explaining this decision to my church. In time, however, I realized that the NKJV also had its fair share of problems, including the capitalization of divine pronouns which I found to be distracting and sometimes misleading. After completing an expositional preaching series using the NKJV, I began a new series using the KJV and have used it ever since.

As I was rethinking my views on text and translation, I was also moving from being an evangelical Calvinist to becoming a confessional Reformed Baptist. I was discovering the Second London Baptist Confession of 1689 with its classic Trinitarianism, distinctive covenant theology, affirmation of the abiding validity of the moral law (including the fourth commandment), advocacy of the ordinary means of grace, articulation of the Regulative Principle of worship, and Particular Baptist ecclesiology. The two transitions converged in the confession's first chapter and eighth paragraph, which, states, in part:

The Old Testament in Hebrew (which was the native language of the people of God of old), and the New Testament in Greek (which at the time of the writing of it was most generally known to the nations), being immediately inspired by God, and by his singular care and providence kept pure in all ages, are therefore authentical; so as in all controversies of religion, the church is finally to appeal to them.

There seemed little doubt to me as to which Biblical text the framers of the confession were referencing when they spoke of the Hebrew and Greek. This is clear from the prooftexts which they chose to uphold and illustrate the doctrine they espoused (e.g., 1 John 5:7 in chapter two, paragraph three "Of God and Of the Holy Trinity"; and Mark 16:16 and Acts 8:37 in chapter twenty-nine, paragraph two "Of Baptism").

There were other things I read that solidified things for me. These included Edward F. Hills' *The King James Version Defended* and Theodore P. Letis' *The Ecclesiastical Text*, especially his critique of B. B. Warfield. Perhaps most influential was reading the two essays by John Owen on Scripture in Volume 16 of his *Collected Works* (Note: I have simplified and abridged these two works in my book *John Owen on Scripture: Authority, Inspiration, Preservation*). I began to refer to my view on the Bible as the Confessional Text position and have been encouraged to hear that others have found this to be a helpful term.

I certainly could not have articulated the Confessional Text position when I was a child in my rural home church. I am not even sure at what age I realized the Bible was not originally written in English! Someone might say that in embracing the Received Text I am just reverting to what I knew as a child or that my convictions are born of nostalgia. I am actually OK with that description. After all, one of the earliest verses I memorized in "Sword Drills" was Proverbs 22:6, "Train up a child in the way he should go: and when he is old, he will not depart from it." Why do I preach from the Received Text? I find it satisfying and winsome on many levels, aesthetically, intellectually, spiritually, theologically. It has given me a sure foundation upon which to exercise my ministry, and it has increased my faith.

Jeffrey T. Riddle (B.A. Wake Forest University; M.Div. Southern Baptist Theological Seminary; Ph.D. Union Presbyterian Seminary) hosts the podcast Word Magazine and is the Pastor of Christ Reformed Baptist Church in Louisa, Virginia. He resides in North Garden, Virginia, with his wife Llewellyn and the younger of his five children.

21

God's Honor, Christ's Glory, and the Church's Good

Christopher Sheffield

When I entered the gospel ministry almost twenty years ago, there were still many things I was trying to work through in my own thinking. Among the myriad of theological and practical matters I faced was the question of what Bible I should use in preaching and teaching. I had grown up in rural southeast Georgia where many pastors still preached from the King James Version, not because they were KJV-Only, but because it was most familiar to them and their people. It was largely for that same reason that I also used the KJV.

Eventually, I began to wonder whether a more modern translation was better suited for ministry today. The English Standard Version was only recently released, and to almost universal acclamation. It was marketed as an "essentially literal" translation and that sounded great to me, so I purchased a copy and began using it from week to week. My first sermon series was through the Gospel of Mark, and it was not long before I came to chapter sixteen and, right there, in the middle of the chapter, were these words in all capital letters: "[SOME OF THE EARLIEST MANUSCRIPTS DO NOT INCLUDE 16:9-20.]"

I was somewhat startled and confused. What did this mean? Why was this statement stuck in the middle of a chapter? And if it was accurate, why were the words of Mark 16:9-20 ever included in the Bible at all? These were questions to which I had to find answers—not only for myself, but for those to whom I ministered. I did not set out to disprove the claims of the modern Critical Text, only to understand them, but as time went on, I became increasingly convinced that the modern Critical Text and the philosophy which undergirded it, was an affront to the honor of God, the glory of Christ, and good of the Church. These three concerns are why I now preach from the traditional Received Text of Scripture and maintain that it is the Word of God to us still today.

For the Honor of God

The first reason I preach and teach from the traditional Received Text is to uphold the honor of God. This, after all, is to be the impetus behind all that we do (1 Corinthians 10:31). I do not doubt that those brethren who have embraced the modern Critical Text are convinced that it is conducive to that same end. I do not wish to denigrate these brethren in any way, but I am convinced that the modern Critical Text and the working assumptions that undergird it are unworthy of the God of the Bible.

The God of Scripture is a sovereign and almighty God. Nothing is free from his sovereign control. He rules all things in the world by "his most holy, wise, and powerful" providence (WSC, 11). The Psalmist declares, "The Lord hath prepared his throne in the heavens; and his kingdom ruleth over all" (Psalm 103:19). This is why the Lord Jesus could assure us that not even something as insignificant as a sparrow falling to the ground could occur but by the will of our Father in heaven (Matthew 10:29-30). It is the same truth which lies at the foundation of our Lord's words in Matthew 5:18, "For verily I say unto you, Till heaven and earth pass, one jot or one tittle shall in no wise pass from the law, till all be fulfilled" and similarly in Luke 16:17, "And it is easier for heaven and earth to pass, than one tittle of the law to fail." Even more emphatic is his saying, "Heaven and earth shall pass away: but my words shall not pass away" (Luke 21:33).

The simple truth taught in these verses is that the scriptures of the Old and New Testaments have been "by [God's] singular care and providence, kept pure in all ages" (WCF, 1.8). In other words, God has faithfully preserved his Word in every age. He has not allowed a single letter to be lost. He has not suffered wicked men to add anything to or take anything from his sacred Word. The Holy Bible, based upon the Masoretic Text of the Hebrew Old Testament and the Received Text of the Greek New Testament, far from being an inferior text riddled with corruption, is a monument to God's faithfulness to his people!

Some will say, "Yes, but one can believe God has been faithful to preserve his Word and still affirm the modern Critical Text." To which I reply, "How?" How can one believe that the Scriptures were indeed preserved by God while also saying that many things found in the traditional Received Text are in fact later additions and corruptions? I maintain it cannot be done. Ultimately, only one of these propositions can stand, and if you affirm the latter, you must necessarily deny the former. This is why I believe the modern Critical Text greatly dishonors the God of Scripture. Can we deny the preservation of Holy Scripture by God without demeaning his glory and honor? Further, if we cannot affirm his preservation of Scripture, what confidence can we have in his ability to keep and preserve anything else? What confidence can we have that he can keep and preserve us unto his heavenly kingdom? Very little, I fear.

Let us not entertain such low views of God. Let us rather insist upon his faithfulness to do all that he has said. Let us say with the Psalmist, "The words of the LORD are pure words: as silver tried in a furnace of earth, purified seven times" (Psalm 12:6) and with the prophet Isaiah, "The grass withereth, the flower fadeth: but the word of our God shall stand for ever" (Isaiah 40:8).

For the Glory of Christ

My second reason for affirming the traditional Received Text of Scripture is to uphold the glory of the Lord Jesus Christ. While we are told by advocates of the modern Critical Text that variants in the readings make no real difference with regard to the doctrine of the New Testament, a careful consideration of the textual data shows that claim to be wanting. Let us consider four key texts of Scripture and mark how the modern Critical Text undermines the deity and glory of the Lord Jesus Christ.

Acts 20:28 - Paul, in bidding farewell to the Ephesian elders, charged them to "Take heed therefore unto yourselves, and to all the flock, over the which the Holy Ghost hath made you overseers, to feed the church of God, which he hath purchased with his own blood." The main text of the ESV reads, "The church of God which he obtained with his own blood" and there are two marginal notes that appear at the bottom of the page. The first of these notes identifies a textual variant, "*of the Lord*" rather than the reading, "of God." This suggestion is based on only four percent of the manuscript evidence. The second note suggests an alternative to the phrase "with his own blood" which would read, "*with the blood of his Own*." This too is based on a minority text tradition. Such marginal notes might not only confuse the immature reader and undermine his confidence in the reliability of Scripture, but they might also constitute a diminished witness to Christ's full deity in Scripture.

Romans 9:5 - Here the question involves the punctuation that is found in the printed Greek editions of the New Testament. Translations that reflect the punctuation in the Received Text read, "Christ came, who is over all, God blessed for ever. Amen." Some translations based on the punctuation found in the modern Critical Text, however, offer a more subdued rendering. The RSV, for example, reads, "... the Christ. God who is over all be blessed for ever. Amen" (RSV). By replacing a comma with a period, the editors of the Critical Text rob our Lord Jesus of that glory justly ascribed to him as "God blessed for ever. Amen."

1 Timothy 3:16 - Here, the Apostle says, "And without controversy great is the mystery of godliness: God was manifest in the flesh, justified in the Spirit, seen of angels, preached unto the Gentiles, believed on in the world, received up into glory." Here we have both a beautiful summary of the gospel of Jesus Christ as well as a clear statement of his deity, but again, the Critical Text ignores

the overwhelming support for the traditional reading and replaces "God" with "he," again favoring an extreme minority of manuscripts that may lend themselves to a denial of Christ's deity.

Revelation 1:8, 11 - The Received Text reads as follows: "I am Alpha and Omega, the beginning and the ending, saith the Lord, which is, and which was, and which is to come, the Almighty... Saying, I am Alpha and Omega, the first and the last." Here, it is obvious that the one speaking is Christ. He refers to himself as "the beginning and the ending," titles that only rightfully belong to God. Further, as the Second Person of the blessed Trinity, Christ is, in the words of the Nicene Creed, affirmed as "The only-begotten Son of God; begotten of his Father before all worlds, God of God, Light of Light, very God of very God; begotten, not made; being of one substance with the Father; by whom all things were made." Sadly, the modern Critical Text reads, "I am the Alpha and the Omega," says the Lord God, "who is and who was and who is to come, the Almighty" (ESV). Adding the word "God" after Lord in verse 8 could possibly be misconstrued as a reference to the Father, rather than to the Son.

While we are confident that there are sincere brethren who uphold these foundational truths while advocating for the Critical Text, we maintain their claim that nothing of any doctrinal significance is changed by the modern Critical Text is untrue. The changes introduced by the Critical Text strike at the very core of the Christian faith—the person of Jesus Christ. Can the deity of Jesus Christ be established by other texts? Of course, but why should we allow any of the Spirit's testimony of Christ to be tossed aside? God forbid! Let us allow nothing of that glorious revelation of the eternal Son of

God be lost to us, because we were spoiled by the vain philosophy of modern text-critical theory. Let us affirm that the Lord Jesus Christ is God, manifested in the flesh, who purchased the church with his own blood, the Alpha and Omega, the beginning and the ending, God blessed for ever. Amen.

For the Good of the Church

The third and final reason I maintain the Received Text as the true Word of God is for the good of God's people—the Church. The Apostle Paul writes to the church at Rome saying, "For whatsoever things were written aforetime were written for our learning, that we through patience and comfort of the scriptures might have hope" (Romans 15:4). It was not only God's will to save sinners from their sins and bring them at last to glory, it was his will that, notwithstanding their trials and tribulations, they would enjoy real and solid comfort through the Holy Scriptures.

When God's people open their Bibles in the morning for prayer, or before the preaching of God's Word on Sunday, it should be an occasion for comfort and consolation in their earthly pilgrimage. It should be a time when their hope and confidence in God are strengthened. Frequently, however, this gracious purpose has been thwarted by the modern Critical Text. With its never-ending number of revisions and translations, which are being continuously revised, the text of Scripture might appear to be in a constant state of flux.

This is not surprising if one is at all acquainted with what advocates of the Critical Text believe. Daniel Wallace is one of the most prominent proponents of the modern Critical Text. In a foreword to the book *Myths and Mistakes in New Testament Textual Criticism*, he declares:

> We do not have now—in our critical Greek texts or any translations—exactly what the authors of the New Testament wrote. Even if we did, we would not know it. There are many, many places in which the text of the New Testament is uncertain" (xii).

There you have it. We do not have the whole Word of God and even if we did, we wouldn't know it. Listen carefully to what he is saying, "There are *many, many* places in which the text of the New Testament is *uncertain*." (emphasis mine). Could there be anything more harmful to the child of God than to have some scholar take a proverbial Sharpie and write a giant question mark over every page of his Bible? That is what the modern Critical Text method does, and it can bear no good fruit in the child of God or in the church of Christ. Such a mindset does not provide patience, comfort, and hope (cf. Romans 15:4), but rather exasperation, anxiety, and despair. It will not produce stable believers with a growing confidence in their Bibles and willingness to labor and suffer for its proclamation, but only the opposite.

For the sake of God's honor, Christ's glory, and the Church's good, let us then abandon this never-ending project of "revision" and heed the admonition of Lord to his people of old, "Thus saith the LORD, Stand ye in the ways, and see, and ask for the old paths, where is the good way, and walk therein, and ye shall find rest for your souls" (Jeremiah 6:16).

Christopher Sheffield (B.B.S. Moody Bible Institute) has served as Pastor of Grace Reformed Baptist Church of Rocky Mount, North Carolina since 2013. He also serves on the Board of Directors for Covenant Baptist Theological Seminary in Owensboro, Kentucky. He and his wife Cynthia have been married since 2003 and have six children.

22

The Absurdity of Modern
Textual Criticism

John Thackway

Christians who believe in a supernaturally given Bible find it a small step also to believe that God has preserved that Bible intact, for "his work is perfect" (Deuteronomy 32:4). Providential preservation does not mean that God has secured to us the original manuscripts of Holy Scripture. For his all-wise reasons, these no longer exist. One writer put it like this, "One can imagine how easily (and quickly) such documents would become objects of veneration, if not worship. They might have become the equivalent of Gideon's ephod (Judges 8:27) — a good gift the people begin to treat as an idol" (from an online article by Michael J. Kruger, 2013).

What providential preservation does mean, however, is that the necessary copying and transmission of these autographs has been divinely guarded from alteration and loss. Our Lord has assured us,

"Heaven and earth shall pass away, but my words shall not pass away" (Matthew 24:35). His word is, "settled in heaven" (Psalm 119:89), and is securely settled upon earth.

Until late in the nineteenth century most of the Lord's people held this high and believing view of Scripture. Already, however, there was an increasing interest in a field of academic study that began to control and undermine confidence in the finality of the Bible. This discipline is called "Modern Textual Criticism" (i.e., the search for the nearest text to the original). It quickly became the guru of New Testament scholarship, not only among theological liberals, but sadly among many conservative evangelicals, and even some Reformed theologians.

Modern textual criticism advances on the premise that providential preservation either did not take place or took place only in a general sense. This approach not only considers that the autographs have been lost, but it also focuses on the numerous copies made over many generations which abound in many corruptions, glosses, and interpolations. These critics concluded that a more authentic Scripture than the traditional text may exist somewhere else in the mass of these manuscripts. Therefore, they suggest that patient, scholarly critical research is needed to sift and collate the more than 5,000 manuscripts, together with the versions (early translations of scripture into other languages), lectionaries (early compiled scripture readings for worship services), and the Fathers (the Scripture quotations the early church leaders used in their writings) to arrive at what *they* believe is the nearest text to the original.

These conclusions are often quite subjective—and pessimistic. Some textual critics have even concluded that the quest is hopeless.

One such, Kirsopp Lake (1872-1946), stated, "We do not know the original form of the Gospels, and it is quite likely that we never shall" (*Family 13*, vii). Another, R.M. Grant (1917-2014), declared, "The recovery of what the New Testament writers wrote... is well-nigh impossible" (*A Historical Introduction to the New Testament*, 51).

A Place for Textual Criticism

That there is a place for textual criticism, rightly understood, we acknowledge. The word "criticism" in this sense means to review and judge the merit of something. The men the Lord used to study and compare the readings found in manuscripts and to bring together the early editions of our Greek New Testament were textual critics in this sense. They included Erasmus (1466-1536), Estienne, also known as Stephanus (1503-1559), Theodore Beza (1519-1605), and the Elzevir family (who published seven editions of the Greek New Testament between 1624 and 1678). It was the Elzevir's second edition in 1633 that had the Latin preface which included the words, "the text which is now received by all," from which has come the title *Textus Receptus* or Received Text (TR).

This text is what underlies the New Testament of the Authorized (King James) Version (AV). Moreover, the men raised up in the nineteenth century to defend this traditional text and the Protestant translations made from it were textual critics of the highest order. They included men like Scrivener, Burgon, Miller—and their counterparts up to our day. True textual criticism believes the work needed is not a potentially hopeless search for the "real" New Testament, but a tidying up and limited clarifying of a few readings. An example of this is Ephesians 6:9, where the AV reads, "your Master" and the margin notes, "Some read, *both your master and their master*." Alan J. Macgregor helpfully explains this:

> It should be noted that it is now difficult to reconstruct the exact Greek text underlying the AV. The translators worked with Theodore Beza's slight revision of Erasmus' fifth edition, but clearly consulted other TR texts. However, the differences are so slight as to be minor variations of the one homogenous text. The TR Greek Text published by the Trinitarian Bible Society is that assumed to underline (sic) the AV, as edited and published by F.H.A. Scrivener in 1894 (*Three Modern Versions: A Critical Assessment of the NIV, ESV and NKJV*, 7, n. 4).

Hijacked

If this were all that was meant by textual criticism, we would not be using the word "absurd" in connection with it. However, the term has been hijacked by those who have given it their own meaning. For such men as Griesbach, Tischendorf, Lachmann, Westcott, and Hort, the term refers to the science whereby Scripture is treated like any other ancient literature. Therefore, we must rely upon their research and conclusions for what is likely to be the most authentic and reliable Greek New Testament text.

This naturalistic, trial and error approach, is evident in the many different and revised editions of the Greek New Testaments such men published. Tischendorf, for instance, had eight editions between 1841 and 1872, declaring his seventh to be final, but then bringing out the eighth with 3,572 changes in it! Textual criticism these days has become something of a compromise, producing an eclectic text which attempts to consider all the available variants. It is this eclectic text that underlies the various modern translations.

Example

Some time ago, an example of the absurdity of modern textual criticism came to light for me while I was preaching a series of sermons on Paul's Epistle to the Ephesians in my congregation at Holywell Evangelical Church. I needed help with Ephesians 5:30, "For we are members of his body, of his flesh, and of his bones." Among the works I consulted were those by William Hendriksen and Marytn Lloyd-Jones. The first was a technical commentary, and the second a series of sermons on that part of Ephesians 5. I was interested to discover that these men clashed over whether half of the verse in question should be there at all. This is what they wrote.

> Hendriksen—Although Hodge, Simpson and others favour the retention of the words "of his flesh, and of his bones" (A.V.), the latter claiming that they have "strong MSS. support," and the former that "they are required by the context," I cannot join their company. The external evidence for their retention does not impress me as being nearly as strong as is that for their omission, and since in the present paragraph the oneness of Christ and his church has been stressed over and over, I do not see that anything is lost when they are left out (*New Testament Commentary: Exposition of Ephesians*, 255, n. 159).

Lloyd-Jones—But that is only introduction. He goes further, and in verse 30 he adds, 'For we are members of His body' – then he makes this extraordinary addition – 'of His flesh, and of His bones'. He is talking about the relationship of the church to the Lord Jesus Christ. It is here that we really enter into the mystery. The notion of the church as the body of Christ, while difficult, is nothing like so difficult as this addition, 'of His flesh, and of His bones'. Some have tried to avoid this altogether by pointing out that in certain manuscripts this addition is not present; but it is generally agreed by all the best authorities that in all the best manuscripts this is present. So we cannot solve the problem in that fashion. And indeed the whole context, and the following quotation from Genesis 2, make it essential that we should keep it here, otherwise there is no point or purpose in the quotation. There, as I shall show he is clearly referring to Genesis 2; and he is certainly doing the same here (*Life in the Spirit: In Marriage, Home & Work: An Exposition of Ephesians*, 187).

Some observations struck me as I read these conflicting statements concerning half a New Testament verse:

First, was the subjective basis of Hendriksen's conclusions: He makes statements like, "I cannot join their company," "does not impress me," and "I do not see that anything is lost." Is the authenticity of our precious New Testament really in the hands of what finite and fallible men think? (cf. Psalm 118:8).

Second, the words in question cause difficulty: As Lloyd-Jones admits, the concept of the church being in mystical union with

Christ, even "of his flesh, and of his bones," is not easy to understand. "The Dr.," however, faced this difficulty and did not cut the knot by simply explaining the words away. I wonder if the very difficulty of these words lay behind some copyists leaving them out in the manuscripts favored by the critical texts, while providentially retained in the Received Text. If so, to depart from providential preservation means that parts of the New Testament are always at the mercy of biased copyists and critics.

Third, these two men contradict each other: Hendriksen would have these seven words (nine in the Greek) left out, because he thinks they are not needed. Lloyd-Jones insists they should be retained; otherwise, the sense of the verse is lost. Whose opinion do we accept? Such contradiction is typical when the Received Text is not the Greek of your New Testament. Hendriksen says he parts company with Charles Hodge, who wrote:

These words are omitted in MSS. A B 17, and in the Coptic and Ethiopic versions, and are left out of the text by Lachmann and Tischendorf. The other Uncial MSS., the Syriac version, the Fathers, are in their favour. They are required by the context, and their omission is easily accounted for. Even Mill and Griesbach retain them, as do all other editors, and the commentators without exception (*Commentary on the Epistle to the Ephesians*, 171, n. 24).

Westcott, however, would have agreed with Hendriksen in his rejection of this phrase. In his posthumous commentary on Ephesians, he cavalierly states, "The words that follow in the common text are an unintelligent gloss, in which an unsuccessful endeavour is made to give greater distinctiveness to the Apostle's statement" (*St. Paul's Epistle to the Ephesians*, 86).

When we add the opinion of Bishop Wordsworth, in his Greek New Testament with notes, unanimity slips further away: "The words ... are not in A, B, and have been rejected by *Lachm., Tisch.*, but they are supported by the great majority of authorities, and are received by *Meyer, Ellicott, Alf.*" (Christian Wordsworth, *Greek New Testament*, Vol. 3, 297).

Such contradictory opinions and their reasons could be multiplied. Whom do we indeed believe? It seems the fate of part of Scripture is in the hands of men who cannot even agree amongst themselves! "God is not the author of confusion" (1 Corinthians 14:33).

Fourth, Hendriksen's standing is even questioned: He has taken the opposite side from many others on the authenticity of these seven words. This is indeed a bold stand. What about Lloyd-Jones' insistence that this phrase "is generally agreed by *all the best authorities*" (emphasis mine)? This would mean that Hendriksen is not one "of the best authorities." But then who is, when it comes to saying what is God's Word and what is not?

Fifth, some of sacred Scripture is taken away: A solemn warning occurs more than once concerning what we do with God's word: "Ye shall not add unto the word which I command you, neither shall ye diminish ought from it" (Deuteronomy 4:2, cf. 12:32; Revelation 22:19). God severely judged that wicked king Jehoiakim, who cut up God's Word with a penknife (Jeremiah 36:23, 29-31). In the light of such things, the casual way men speak of leaving in or out part of God's Word seems vastly different from the spirit expressed by Isaiah, describing that one who "is poor and of a contrite spirit, and trembleth at my word" (Isaiah 66:2).

These seven words are not all that is disputed in Ephesians by modern textual critics. When the Received Text is compared with the Nestle-Aland 26 (a modern critical text underlying many modern translations) it shows that fifteen words are missing from the whole of Ephesians chapter 5, and forty-one from the whole epistle! If you compare the entire the New Testament in the Nestle Aland text with the Received Text, one finds that the modern critical text is shorter by 2,886 words, which is about the number of words in 1 and 2 Peter! (Taken from an online article by Jack A. Moorman).

ESV and NKJV

I thought it would be an interesting exercise to see what two of the most commonly used English translations do with this verse, so I consulted the English Standard Version and the New King James Version. The ESV leaves out these seven words with no explanation whatsoever. The NKJV retains them but then raises doubts over their authenticity in the marginal note, "NU [the modern critical text] omits the rest of v. 30."

Surely God's people want a Bible that they know is God's Word in its *entirety*, not one that has parts of its New Testament either excised, or accepted in a qualified fashion. The absurdity of textual criticism leaves us in an absurd position regarding the Word of God. However, with belief in providential preservation in our hearts, and the traditional text in our hands, we can be confident that we have "the word of God, which liveth and abideth for ever" (1 Peter 1:23).

Conclusion

So, what did I do about those seven words in Ephesians 5:30? I simply accepted them as inspired and preserved Scripture, prepared the sermon, and preached it. I can honestly say that I felt a special unction from the Holy Spirit upon the ministry that Lord's Day morning!

John Thackway (Dipl. Bible Training Institute, Glasgow Scotland) is minister of Emmanuel Church, Salisbury, UK, editor of the Bible League Quarterly, Vice-Chairman of the General Committee of the Trinitarian Bible Society, trustee and lecturer at the Salisbury Reformed Seminary. He is married to Margaret, and they have four children and seven grandchildren.

23

The Received Text is the Canonical Text

Robert Truelove

The question of the proper text of the New Testament is similar to the question of which books belong within it. The question we are seeking to answer in relation to both is, "Is this Scripture?" On both fronts, this is a question of canonicity. "Is this Scripture?" is a *canonical* question, whether we are asking it of a book, or even of a particular reading within a canonical book. Under the term canon, we recognize what is (and what is not) authoritative Scripture. The historical process in which God's people came to recognize the canon is what we call canonization.

A naturalistic view of canonization explains this process as merely a human endeavor. This view sees the canon as simply the result of human psychology and a community's unique place in history. It is grounded in unbelief and is therefore not a Christian understanding.

To distinguish the books from the text of those books, I employ the terms "macro-canon" (books) and "micro-canon" (text). As we shall see, these are related, though different. For instance, it is senseless to speak of the canonical readings of any particular book without first recognizing that the book itself is canonical. When I answer the question of why I preach from translations of the Received Text, I am answering a canonical question.

It is ultimately the work of the Holy Spirit, authenticating the Scriptures upon the hearts of believers, that leads one to recognize and receive the canon of scripture. This has resulted in the acceptance of those books and texts that are Scripture by God's people and the rejection of those that are not. This is the Bible's own teaching on the matter. It is telling that the Bible itself contains no authoritative list of scriptures and yet the biblical authors clearly recognized the scriptures in their own day. Consider, for example, these statements from David and Paul: "O how love I thy law! It is my meditation all the day" (Psalm 119:97) and "All scripture is given by inspiration of God, and is profitable for doctrine, for reproof, for correction, for instruction in righteousness" (2 Timothy 3:16).

What the Biblical authors were receiving as Scripture in their own day was that which had been already received as Scripture by those who had come before them. This was not a human development, but the work of God giving, authenticating, and preserving those same scriptures for the benefit of his church. When God speaks, the Holy Spirit authenticates his word in the hearts and minds of believers. As Christ said, "My sheep hear my voice, and I know them, and they follow me..." (John 10:27). While the believing community does play a role in the canonization process, it is not merely a human affair. It is not the ruling of the church that authenticates Scripture, but the testimony of the Holy Spirit.

The Place of Epistemology

How we understand canonization flows from our epistemology (i.e., how we know what we know). As believers, we confess that the scriptures are themselves the ultimate authority for all matters pertaining to faith and practice (WCF and LBCF, 1.8). The scriptures are themselves the very words of God (2 Timothy 3:16).

A naturalistic view of the canon places the scriptures under the authority of man as authenticator. This is antithetical to a biblically informed epistemology. Such an approach envisions the process of canonization as the decisions of man based upon time, culture, circumstances and, in the case of contemporary textual criticism, human reason.

The Roman Catholic view is that the church is the arbiter of what is or is not Scripture. This approach makes the church the authenticating authority and places Scripture under the church. As Protestants, however, we confess that the scriptures are self-authenticating by the power of the Holy Spirit (WCF and LBCF, 1.5). This is consistent with a biblical epistemology, which places everything under the authority of the Word of God, acknowledging the scriptures as the final authority for faith and practice.

Recognizing the Macro-Canon

Let us first consider the question of how the macro-canon (books) was recognized. The majority of evangelical scholars will admit that most of the books in the New Testament were universally recognized as scripture from the very beginning. These books are sometimes referred to as the *homolegoumena* (i.e., the undisputed books). On the other hand, some books were disputed for many centuries. Scholars refer to these as the *antilegomena* (i.e., the books "spoken against"). These disputed books included Hebrews, James, 2 Peter, 2 and 3 John, Jude, and Revelation. Though disputed, these books were eventually and universally recognized as authentic Scripture. This stands in contrast to books that were rejected as non-canonical including, the Gospel of the Hebrews, the Apocalypse of Peter, the Acts of Paul, the Shepherd of Hermas, the Epistle of Barnabas, and the Didache.

While many of the questions pertaining to the macro-canon were cleared up within the first few centuries of Christianity, there were lingering questions over the *antilegomena* that lasted all the way up until the time of the Reformation. For example, in Martin Luther's German Bible, he placed the books of Hebrews, James, Jude, and Revelation in the back and cast doubt upon their canonicity in his preface.

Recognizing the Micro-Canon

When we look at the micro-canon (texts), we find that there were also questions over the correct form of the text. There were questions over the status of translations. For example, the Eastern church recognized the Septuagint as canonical for the Old Testament, and the Roman Catholic Church, at the Council of Trent, decreed that the Latin Vulgate was authoritative for both testaments. On the other hand, there were always believers who recognized that the scriptures were immediately inspired in the Hebrew Old Testament and the Greek New Testament, and thus gave preference to those.

There were also questions regarding the transmission of the text. Scribal errors and alterations had crept into some of the handwritten copies which predated the printing press. Some of the textual variants were minor, while others involved lengthy passages, such as the resurrection account in Mark's Gospel (Mark 16:9-20) and the woman caught in adultery in John's Gospel (John 7:53-8:11).

Unbelievers have a tendency to overstate the difficulty that these historical questions of macro and micro-canon may pose for the Christian faith. When it comes to the New Testament, we have already seen how quickly and universally most of the books were acknowledged as canon. The idea that the Bible is a product of the church several centuries removed from the Apostles is specious. On the other hand, many believers have the tendency to understate some of these problems. Many popular books defending the Bible give the impression that all questions pertaining to the recognition of canon were resolved by the third or fourth century. This was simply not the case.

The Protestant View

The reason it is important for us to have a biblical view of the canon is so that we can more accurately appreciate what the Holy Spirit has done in authenticating the scriptures he himself inspired. Otherwise, questions of canon will continue to linger forever, which is not consistent with the Protestant Reformed view.

The significance of the Protestant Reformation cannot be overstated. It proved to be the most significant event in church history since the time of the Apostles. This is true with regard to a great many things, including the Christian canon. By the middle of the sixteenth century, the lingering questions pertaining to the canon were put to rest. For the first time in history and in response to the Reformation, Rome would hold an ecumenical council (Trent 1545-1563) and formally reject the gospel of justification by faith alone. Also at this council, Rome approved the canonical status of the Apocrypha and adopted the Latin Vulgate as the authoritative form of the text.

The Protestants, however, confessed the thirty-nine books of the Hebrew Old Testament and the twenty-seven books of the Greek New Testament to be canonical. We find this in many writings of the Reformers, and it is formally stated in their confessions. For example, the Belgic Confession (1561) lists the sixty-six books of the Protestant canon and explicitly rejects the canonical status of the Apocrypha. The Westminster Confession (1646), along with the Savoy Declaration (1658), and the London Baptist Confession of Faith (1677/1689) affirm the same. They also recognized the canonical form of the Scriptures in the original languages of Hebrew and Greek.

The invention of the printing press in 1450 and the printing of the Greek New Testament in 1516 by Erasmus of Rotterdam led to the general acceptance of that particular form of the text by the Protestants. This "Received Text" largely reflected the text that had been in general use for centuries by the Greek-speaking church. Many Roman Catholic scholars challenged this text, suggesting that the Hebrew and Greek original had been corrupted and needed to be properly interpreted by the Roman magisterium. The Protestant theologians defended these traditional texts, especially on dogmatic grounds.

One of the principal arguments used in defense of the Received Text was the providential preservation of the scriptures. The chief minds of the Reformation viewed the older manuscripts of the Greek New Testament that did not conform to the Received Text as early corruptions. Of primary concern was the fact that God had preserved his inspired Word by his special care and providence, and kept it pure in all ages. When contending with those who would multiply textual variants in the New Testament, John Owen wrote:

> It can, then, with no colour of probability be asserted (which yet I find some learned men too free in granting), namely, that there hath the same fate attended the Scripture in its transcription, as hath done other books. Let me say without offence, this imagination, asserted on deliberation, seems to me to border on atheism. Surely the promise of God for the preservation of his word, with his love and care of his church, of whose faith and obedience that word of his is the only rule, requires other thoughts at our hands (*Collected Works*, Vol. 16, 357).

As for the Received Text, in the same treatise, Owen declares (emphasis added):

> Let it be remembered that the vulgar copy we use, was the public possession of many generations,—that upon the invention of printing it was in actual authority throughout the

world with them that used and understood that language, as far as anything appears to the contrary; *let that, then, pass for the standard, which is confessedly its right and due*, and we shall, God assisting, quickly see how little reason there is to pretend such varieties of readings as we are now surprised withall... (*Collected Works*, Vol. 16, 366).

The Received Text was also vindicated in the Reformed confessions and catechisms. 1 John 5:7 is cited as a proof text for the Holy Trinity, and the last question of the Shorter Catechism affirms the authenticity of Matthew 6:13b as the conclusion of the Lord's Prayer (WCF 2, WSC 107). Though there were critics at the time who rejected such texts, this did not stop the framers of the confessions from using them.

The Received Text would continue to be recognized as the canonical text by most Protestants up until the late-nineteenth century when Post-Enlightenment thought would challenge the epistemological commitments of the Reformation. The "Age of Reason" began to influence Christians to view the Bible along more naturalistic grounds. This shift was recognized by Kurt Aland, one of the most influential textual critics of the twentieth century:

Finally it is undisputed that from the 16th to the 18th century orthodoxy's doctrine of verbal inspiration assumed this Textus Receptus. It was the only Greek text they knew, and they regarded it as the "original text" (*Trinity Journal*, 1987, 131).

Yet no real progress was possible as long as the Textus Receptus remained the basic text and its authority was regarded as canonical (*The Text of the New Testament*, 6).

It is my contention that the recognition of the macro-canon and micro-canon at the time of the Reformation was not a mere "accident of history." I share John Owen's concern that to reject the authenticity of the original text "borders on atheism." This was the time in Christian history when any lingering questions pertaining to the canon were decisively answered by God himself via special providence.

A theological distinction must be made between general and special providence. This distinction is made by the Westminster and London Baptist Confessions as follows: "As the providence of God doth in general reach to all creatures, so after a more special manner it taketh care of his church, and disposeth of all things to the good thereof" (5.7). I find it both stunning and obvious that at the time in history when the Lord was reforming his church, and bringing his people to submit to the authority of the Bible alone, that the lingering questions of both the macro-canon and the micro-canon were decisively settled. Many thousands of God's people all over the world continue to know the Holy Spirit's vindication of the Received Text. I preach from the Received Text because the text of Scripture is a canonical concern and the Holy Spirit alone is the authenticator of the canon. The Received Text is the Canonical Text.

Robert Truelove is Pastor of Christ Reformed Church in Lawrenceville, Georgia. He and his wife Patricia have four children.

24

The Approach, Attack, and Animosity of Modern Textual Criticism

J. D. "Doc" Watson

Like most every man in ministry today, I was taught that the modern translations of the Bible are the best, because they were "based on the oldest and therefore the most accurate Hebrew and Greek manuscripts." That is what I believed and what I then taught when I entered ministry. If confronted occasionally with another view (i.e., the superiority of the KJV and its underlying Hebrew and Greek texts), I was trained to ignore such things as the ramblings of ignorant, naïve simpletons.

One Sunday morning around 1991, however, I made this statement in my sermon about a particular verse, "The older and more reliable manuscripts say this." After the service, a visitor, whom I already knew and respected for his scholarly biblical knowledge, came up to me and said, "You know, you might want to take a look at what is called the Majority Text Theory. It basically says that the reading found in the majority of manuscripts is more important than the reading found in the so-called older manuscripts."

I was dumb-founded. Here was a guy that I positively knew was not an ignorant, naïve simpleton. So, I began studying the issue from both sides. A contributing factor to my study was an increasing burden I was experiencing at the time over the waning of the doctrines of biblical authority and sufficiency. The more I studied, the more I understood what that really meant. Further, the more I understood that, the more I realized that the issue of Bible texts and translations is, in fact, inseparably connected to them. What I found stunned me.

In all my research and writing on this issue, three observations have most affected me and well summarize why I hold to the Traditional Text (a.k.a., Received Text or Ecclesiastical Text) and preach from it. All three relate to modern textual criticism:

Its Underlying Approach to Scripture

Due to limited space, I jump to the core issue, which is the underlying approach modern textual criticism takes to reconstructing the original text and its underlying attitude toward the Bible itself: *the method of restoring the original text of Scripture is no different than for any other kind of literature*. That has been stated plainly by many, such as Norman Geisler and William Nix (cf. *General Introduction to the Bible*, Revised and Expanded, 433, 435, 465). In short, they state that the point of textual criticism is to study the various manuscripts that *do* exist of *any* literary work (the Bible in this case) and recreate as closely as possible the original text that *no longer* exists.

While that approach may seem reasonable, even noble, it is founded on a fundamental error: it treats the text of Scripture like any other kind of literature when Scripture is *not* like any other kind of literature. Beginning with Johann A. Bengel, who was succeeded by Johann J. Griesbach and J.S. Semler (the "Father of German Rationalism"), this idea was passed down to a long string of others who all agree on that essential point (e.g., Johann L. Hug, Martin L. Scholtz, Karl Lachmann, Lobegott F.C. von Tischendorf, etc.).

Of special note is Samuel P. Tregelles "who was chiefly instrumental in leading England away from the *Textus Receptus* during the mid-nineteenth century" (Geisler and Nix, 455). Additionally, Henry Alford is well known for his desire for "the demolition of the unworthy and pedantic reverence for the Received Text, which stood in the way of all chance of discovering the genuine word of God" ("Prolegomena," *The Greek Testament*, 1:76). The pattern here is unmistakable. From the modern era forward, the concept of an already existing, divinely preserved, definitive text of the New Testament was rejected. The baton then passed to two Cambridge scholars, Brooke F. Westcott and Fenton J.A. Hort, and Christianity has never been the same since. Not only did they believe that orthodox scribes altered the text (as did Bengel and the rest)—this basically means the scribes *lied*—but Hort added:

In dealing with the text of the New Testament no new principle whatever [such as God's providential preservation] is needed or legitimate... We dare not introduce considerations which could not reasonably be applied to other ancient texts (*The New Testament in the Original Greek*, 73, 277).

It is unambiguously clear that such an idea was not born of God's revelation, but was the spawn of German rationalism. Tragically, it does not bother most Christians that woven through the very fabric of modern textual criticism, from Bengel to the present day, is the belief that it was not God who *preserved* the true text by sovereign providence, but it is we who must *procure* the true text by rational means. To say it another way, instead of there being a text that has been *recognized* down through the ages as the preserved text of God's Word (the Traditional, or Ecclesiastical Text), it is up to man to *reconstruct* the original text, whatever that might be. Frankly, after thirty years of studying this issue, I simply do not understand how evangelicals can defend German rationalism and an approach to Scripture that dishonors the sovereign providence of God.

Its Unconscionable Attack on Infallibility

An issue that is rarely addressed, even by defenders of the Traditional Text, is that of the damage done by B.B. Warfield. While unquestionably one of the church's greatest defenders of the faith (and I in no way want to detract from that), he nevertheless helped change the doctrine of verbal inspiration. After returning from Germany, where he studied textual criticism under German rationalists, he virtually turned his back on that doctrine. His view changed to that of Westcott and Hort, namely, that when reconstructing any text, the same method should be applied, "Whether the writing before us be a letter from a friend, or an inscription from Carchemish, or a copy of a morning newspaper, or Shakespeare, or Homer, or the Bible" (B.B. Warfield, *Introduction to Textual Criticism*, 10).

Further, a shocking, virtually unconscionable move by Warfield was his reinterpreting a statement in the *Westminster Confession of Faith* (WCF) to actually "prove" the validity of rationalistic textual criticism. The confession reads:

> The Old Testament in Hebrew... and the New Testament in Greek... being immediately inspired by God, and, by his singular care and providence, kept pure in all ages, are therefore authentical... so as, in all controversies of religion, the church is finally to appeal unto them (WCF, 1.8).

Here, then, is what Warfield wrote in 1891 about that statement:

> As to the former matter, the Confession (sect. 8) asserts that the final appeal in all controversies is to be made to the original Hebrew and Greek Scriptures, which are alone safeguarded in their accuracy by divine inspiration, and it asserts that these originals have been, "by God's singular care and providence, kept pure in all ages" (*Selected Shorter Writings*, Vol. 2, 569).

What's wrong with his emphasis on final appeal being made only to the "original" inspired manuscripts? Only that the Confession had *never* been interpreted that way in over two centuries.

Theodore P. Letis, a credentialed church historian, did extensive research on Warfield. He wrote of Warfield's "ingenious new interpretation" of the Confession, namely, that while it "had once taught the providential *preservation* of the extant Church texts, [it] was now used to affirm the providential *restoration* of an inerrant original text, by means of modern text criticism" (*The Ecclesiastical Text*, 22). In other words, before Warfield's reinterpretation, the Confession had *always* referred to faithful copies of the Greek texts as being inspired, *not just the originals*. Warfield's incorrect reinterpretation of the Confession, in fact, is now mimicked by virtually every evangelical today.

History also convincingly demonstrates that from the post-apostolic church, through the Reformation, and right up to the end of the nineteenth century, anyone who defended the authority of Scripture always defended an *extant edition* of the Bible as a sacred infallible text. In fact, up to the time of Warfield, the term "inerrancy" was *never* used in reference to the Bible. Rather, the much stronger term "infallible" was invariably utilized. As the WCF again states, "The infallible rule of interpretation of Scripture is the Scripture itself." Another example was the great seventeenth century theologian Francis Turretin, who wrote this about extant manuscripts:

> By the original texts we do not mean the autographs written by the hand of Moses, or the prophets, and the apostles, which certainly do not now exist. We mean their apographs [copies] which are so called because they set forth to us the Word of God in the very words of those who wrote under the immediate inspiration of the Holy Spirit... the autographs and also the accurate and faithful copies may be the standard of all other copies of the same writing and of its translations (*Institutes of Elenctic Theology*, Vol. 1, 106, 113).

It was the doctrine of *infallibility* that Turretin defended. Not once in his writings do we find the word *inerrancy*. Space prohibits similar quotations from the great Puritan John Owen, but he also defended the *apographs* as well as the *autographs*. After doing so, in fact, he added twelve arguments for why all this is true. The first five, in brief, are:

> 1. The *providence of God* in taking care of his word... 2. The *religious care* of the church... 3. The care of the first writers in giving out *authentic copies*... 4. The *multiplying copies* to such a number that it was impossible any should corrupt them all, willfully or by negligence; 5. The preservation of the *authentic* copies... (*The Works of John Owen*, XVI, 358).

Owen's statements are extremely important. He speaks of God's *providence*, not man's *presumptuousness*. He speaks of the *care* of the church, not the *confusion* of men. He speaks of *authentic* copies, not *anemic* copies. What we oppose today is what Owen fought against over three hundred years ago!

So, when did the term "inerrant" come into use? As Letis outlines, as the twentieth century drew near, Warfield felt threatened by liberal textual criticism. The critics argued that because of textual variations, there was no longer an "infallible" Bible. Warfield looked at the manuscripts and agreed that there were variations, so he wondered how he should respond. While he still held to verbal inspiration, he felt the need to make an adjustment to his teaching. The adjustment was that he would no longer defend any extant edition as being infallible. Instead, he would contend that the original autographs were perfect, better than any extant copies or printed editions of them.

In formulating his new position, Warfield used a brand new term, "inerrancy," which he actually borrowed from astronomy, a term that refers to the planets as they orbit "inerrantly," that is, without deviation. He sincerely believed this would silence the critics. If they pointed out some discrepancy or variant reading, he would merely say, "Oh, but we're not defending this copy; we're defending the original autographs as inerrant."

The problems with this approach should be obvious. First, he was defending something that was no longer extant. Second, in the final analysis, he denied the very thing he was trying to defend: the integrity of Scripture. No text of Scripture that now exists is *either* inerrant *or* infallible. Warfield traded something that *does* exist (faithful copies) for something that *does not* (inerrant autographs), a terrible trade indeed. It is because of this shift that virtually every evangelical and fundamentalist today talks about "the inerrant autographs" instead of "the infallible Bible that exists in extant manuscripts." Mark this well: *Inerrancy* always refers to the original autographs, that is, non-extant manuscripts. In stark contrast, *infallibility* was always used to refer to faithful copies, even as far back as the Reformation.

Its Unwarranted Animosity Toward the Traditional Text

Through the years, I have been deeply grieved by those who have displayed open animosity toward the Traditional Text and even scoffed at those who defend it. This actually began with Westcott and Hort, especially the latter, who was mainly responsible for the new Critical Text Theory. At the arrogant age of only twenty three, he called the *Textus Receptus* "villainous" and "vile" (*Life and Letters*, Vol. I, 211), because it was, in his opinion, based on late manuscripts. As Ernest C. Colwell, a leading textual critic of the 1950s and 1960s, wrote: "Hort organized his entire argument to depose the *Textus Receptus*" ("Hort Redivivus," *Studies in methodology in textual criticism of the New Testament*, 158). He elsewhere adds, "Westcott and Hort wrote with two things constantly in mind: the *Textus Receptus* and the *Codex Vaticanus*. But they did not hold them in mind with that passive objectivity which romanticists ascribe to the scientific mind" ("Genealogical Method: Its Achievements and its Limitations," *Journal of Biblical Literature*, LXVI [1947], 111). Everything Hort did, in fact, was subjectively based and deliberately contrived to overthrow the *Textus Receptus*.

That attitude has continued. Textual critics have always relegated the Traditional Text to a "second class citizen" status and rejected it with an almost flippant disregard. This is again due mainly to Hort who claimed a total absence of distinctively Byzantine readings before the mid-fourth century. That, however, was convincingly challenged by Harry Sturtz in his book, *The Byzantine Text-Type and New Testament Textual Criticism*, in which he documented one hundred and fifty distinctively Byzantine readings prior to AD 350 using the papyri. Hort himself maintained that if such readings were ever found, his entire hypothesis would be demolished—*yet it still lives*.

As a result, even the world class scholars who defend the Traditional Text are dismissed out of hand and even mocked. They are often lumped together into an all-inclusive "King James Only" camp, an unconscionable generalization. This includes: John Burgon (a contemporary of Westcott and Hort who exposed their errors),

Edward Miller (Burgon's coworker), Herman Hoskier (who collected a vast amount of devastating data showing the unreliability of *Vaticanus* and *Sinaiticus*), Edward Freer Hills, and others. Hills, in fact (who earned a doctoral degree in textual criticism from Harvard), was the first contemporary textual scholar to approach the text from a *godly theological perspective*, instead of a *skeptically rational* one. While Hills was called naïve and antiquated in his thinking, he uncompromisingly and unconditionally recognized God's sovereign providence over everything. Is that not what evangelicals are supposed to believe?

J.D. "Doc" Watson (D.R.E. Florida Institute of Biblical Studies; Th.D. Golden State School of Theology) has authored sixteen books, edits the bi-monthly publication Truth on Tough Texts, *serves on the board of the Institute for Biblical Textual Studies, and is the Pastor of Grace Bible Church in Meeker, Colorado, where he resides with his wife.*

25

Why Advocate for the
Received Text?

Joshua White

As a Reformed Baptist Pastor, I am often asked the question, "Why do you advocate for and use translations based on the Received Text?" To be certain, I fully understand why the question is being asked. One only has to do a cursory search on the subject of textual criticism to find a great many dear and committed saints of God who not only do not hold to this position but reject it outright. While there seems to be a resurgence of Pastors and church leaders in the West who have begun to advocate for the Received Text, our numbers pale in comparison to the academically-backed opinions on the subject today.

Having been brought up in a conservative Pastor's home and raised in a Baptist church that held to the doctrines of God's sovereign grace, the King James Version of the Bible was used in personal, family, and corporate worship. As a child we were required to memorize Scripture from the aforementioned translation of Scripture. I was introduced to the arguments against modern translations at a young age, and never found myself questioning the veracity of such arguments.

One might think that my background lent itself to the position I now hold regarding the traditional text of Scripture. However, as happens in the lives of most young men, when faced with alternative reasoning, assumptions, and arguments from that which we have always held to be true, early in ministry I found myself having doubts about the text I had revered for so long.

Most of the challenges I faced at that time regarded the Greek text of the New Testament. My first "battle" came as a graduate student working on my ministerial degree. I was quickly and often faced with the question of why it was that I used an antiquated translation based upon an imperfect, even corrupt Greek text. Being the "odd man out," I began to wonder if the many different translations that had come out since the time of my youth had something that the translation I was using did not. Going further, I wondered, "Did the curators of the Critical Text have something more, even better than the translators of yesteryear? If it were true that the Greek text from which my translation came had been added to and corrupted, then how could I have confidence in a translation from it?"

My second "battle" came after I was sent out by my church in Texas to help in the planting and constitution of the Reformed Baptist Church of Elizabethtown, Kentucky. Very early on, it was decided that only translations from the Received Text of Scripture would be used from the pulpit. Within a couple of years, however, there was an effort made to suggest that the Received Text was subpar in light of modern discoveries, and, as a result, the Critical Text should be embraced.

These two "battles" convinced me that the subject of textual criticism is not simply a conflict of ideas, but comes with very practical ramifications. This conviction was only bolstered by my study of the subject at hand. The curators of the Critical Text would have us believe that the church did not have the Word of God in hand with the same clarity we now have in modern critical editions. However, this claim seems to be a little more than suspect. Since the Critical Text was brought to the world stage in the 1880s, the curators of this text have made some very bold statements concerning the Scriptures that were available to and used by the people of the Lord Jesus Christ in personal, family, and corporate worship throughout history.

Those familiar with the subject are acquainted with Bruce Metzger. One cannot enter the halls of religious academia without encountering his voluminous work on the Greek texts of Scripture. Many conservative Christians, however, do not know or understand that Metzger held that every copy of the scriptures that came before the discovery of the manuscripts used to compile the Critical Text were, in fact, corrupt: "It was the corrupt Byzantine form of text that provided the basis for almost all translations of the New Testament into the modern languages down to the nineteenth century" (*A Textual Commentary on the Greek New Testament*, Corrected Edition, xxiii). For those who uphold the Word of God as the sole authority for all faith and practice, this statement by a leading authority on modern textual criticism should cause some concern.

If we look to what was written by another leading curator of the Critical Text in the twentieth century, we have even greater cause for concern:

> If the catholic (*general*) epistles were really written by the apostles whose names they bear and by people who were closest to Jesus, then the real question arises: was there really a Jesus? Can Jesus really have lived, if the writings of his closest companions are filled with so little of his reality? The catholic epistles, for example, have so little in them of the reality of the historical Jesus and his power, that it suffices for James, for example, to mention only Christ's name in passing... When we observe this—assuming that the writings about which we are speaking really come from their alleged authors—it almost then appears as if Jesus were a mere phantom and that the real theological power lay not with him, but with the apostles and with the earthly church (Kurt Aland, *A History of Christianity*, Vol. 2, 106).

The quote above does not specifically mention textual criticism, but it most certainly questions the authority of the Word of God. This comes from a man whose name is prominently attached to the modern Critical Text (the Nestle-Aland edition), which is the basis of popular translations such as the English Standard Version. Ultimately, the paradigm that was used by Aland in the quote above reflects the mindset of those who composed the modern Critical Text. When I discovered this, I became convinced that a significant shift had taken place in the doctrine of scripture, which had also affected the entire evangelical world. No longer was it the church serving as the proper curator of holy writ, but this task had been subcontracted out to those who were unorthodox.

What the curators of the Critical Text advocate is a separation of faith from textual criticism and the treatment of the text of Scripture as any other work of antiquity. They then apply arbitrary rules such as, "the shortest readings are the best readings," or "the oldest manuscript is the best manuscript." In contrast to this, however, we find that the Word of God is self authenticating, and that God has made promises concerning the veracity of his Word and its tenacity. In other words, the canon of Scripture is not like any other book in the world. This realization alarmed me, but it also led me to understand that the Critical Text and all subsequent translations from it are fruit from a poisonous tree, "for whatsoever is not of faith is sin" (Romans 14:23). By not separating faith from textual criticism, the issue was made simpler for me. This led me to ask, "What does the Word of God say about this issue?" This question was then followed up with another, "Has this battle been fought before within the church?"

What Does God Say About This Issue?

He has much to say! How often it is in Scripture that we find the prophets of old affirming that it was indeed the Spirit of God who spoke to them and guided their messages to the people. David's last official word to his kingdom began with, "The Spirit of the LORD spake by me, and his word was in my tongue" (2 Samuel 23:2). We see the very same thing in the major writing prophets of Israel when Isaiah writes as he testifies of God's message concerning the coming

Redeemer, "Come ye near unto me, hear ye this; I have not spoken in secret from the beginning; from the time that it was, there am I: and now the Lord GOD, and his Spirit, hath sent me" (Isaiah 48:16). Of course, there are many other scriptures that make this point.

As the Word of God continued to be revealed, we find that apostolic doctrine further affirmed as true what the prophets of old had written. Peter expressed this very clearly when he wrote, "For the prophecy came not in old time by the will of man: but holy men of God spake as they were moved by the Holy Ghost" (2 Peter 1:21). Paul further explains that within the revealed Word of God through the writers of the Old Testament, the hope that we have in Christ Jesus is made clear, "For whatsoever things were written aforetime were written for our learning, that we through patience and comfort of the scriptures might have hope" (Romans 15:4). What Paul wrote to the Roman church concerning the hope we find in Scripture is precisely what was expressed in Psalm 102:18, "This shall be written for the generation to come: and the people which shall be created shall praise the LORD."

The plain truth is, that if the curators of the modern Critical Text that were quoted above are correct, then Paul could not have said to Timothy, "All scripture is given by inspiration of God, and is profitable for doctrine, for reproof, for correction, for instruction in righteousness: That the man of God may be perfect, thoroughly furnished unto all good works" (2 Timothy 3:16-17). According to modern textual criticism, Christians during the first eighteen hundred years of church history were simply following the errant grammatical expressions of various scribes.

Has This Battle Been Fought Before?

Yes! These doctrinal battles are nothing new to the church. Certainly, there is nothing new under the sun. Many godly men of the past have also fought this good fight.

One such man was a pious Scottish Pastor named Samuel Rutherford, who lived during the seventeenth century. While writing of the early Christian martyrs, he explained that they trusted in the faithful copies of the immediately inspired Word of God and therefore did not forfeit their lives for "mere conjectures and opinions" or something as vain as "the faith of men's fallible skill in grammar, printing and writing" (*A Free Disputation*, 334).

Another worthy opponent of the idea that the Word of God is corrupted and has a need for restoration, was John Owen. As a seventeenth century English nonconformist church leader and theologian, he too wrote in defense of Scripture:

> It can, then, with no colour of probability be asserted (which yet I find some learned men too free in granting), namely, that there hath the same fate attended the Scripture in its transcription as hath done other books. Let me say without offence, this imagination, asserted on deliberation, seems to me to border on atheism. Surely the promise of God for the preservation of his word, with his love and care of his church, of whose faith and obedience that word of his is the only rule, requires other thoughts at our hands (*Collected Works*, Vol. 16, 173-174).

Both Samuel Rutherford and John Owen addressed the very

issue that the church is facing today. With such company as men like these, and with the overwhelming internal evidence of Scripture itself, it became apparent to me that while those who advocate for the Received Text of Scripture are in the minority in our day and age, we must take great care not to be swayed into a paradigm that seeks the restoration of something that has been kept pure by the singular care and providence of God.

As a Minister of the gospel of the Lord Jesus Christ, I can study, counsel, and preach with confidence that I am expounding the very Word of God revealed to his people for his glory. I can also encourage the people under my pastoral care to use the scriptures for personal, family, and corporate worship with every confidence that it is the preserved Word of God to them. This is a confidence that the Critical Text advocate cannot offer. To those who believe that God has providentially preserved his Word, the question of the veracity and tenacity of Scripture has been asked and answered. God has spoken!

Joshua White (B.S. Liberty University; M.C.M. Wayland Baptist University) is the editor of The Sovereign Grace Messenger website, a board member of the Church Assistance Committee with the Sovereign Grace Baptist Fellowship, and Pastor of Reformed Baptist Church of Elizabethtown, Kentucky, where he resides with his wife of twenty years and their four children.

Appendix

Steps Toward Change
in Your Church

Jeffrey T. Riddle & Christian M. McShaffrey

There has been a significant revival of interest in the authentic text of the Hebrew and Greek Scriptures over the past several years. This renewal of interest has occurred, at least in part, due to publications from organizations like the Trinitarian Bible Society; conferences like the Text and Canon Conference (Georgia, 2019) and the Kept Pure in All Ages Conference (Wisconsin, 2021); and internet resources (i.e., blogs, vlogs, podcasts, websites, and social media groups) such as "Young, Textless, and Reformed," "Text & Translation," "Confessional Bibliology," "Reformed Bibliology," and "Word Magazine." Another explanation for this renewed interest might be the acceleration of contemporary text critical work due to advancements in technology (e.g., the Coherence-Based Genealogical Method).

You are probably reading this book because you have some interest in the topic, and perhaps you are now leaning toward the Traditional Text position. Perhaps you are even convinced that it best accords with the teaching of Holy Scripture and the confessions of the historic Protestant Church. If this is true, then you may sense that you now have a lot of work to do in your local church. We hope the counsel offered in this appendix will make that work a little easier.

Advice to the Average Church Member

The truth of divine preservation is one of the most comforting things a Christian can discover. It can also be one of the most disconcerting, since you will find yourself (at least at the present time) holding to a minority position. It is therefore important to stay calm, charitable, and proceed carefully.

Step one: Give a gift. If you are not in a position of church leadership, but a member who would like to see the church reconsider its position on the text of scripture, simply offer a free copy of this book to your Pastor and tell him how much you profited from it spiritually. Do not ask him to read it (because he already has a stack of books "assigned" by well-meaning members), but just offer it as a free gift and follow up with him later.

Step two: Buy him lunch. A couple months after the gift has been given, follow-up with your Pastor and ask if you could meet for lunch to discuss the book. If he confesses to not having read it, say something like, "I'm sorry, I know you have a lot to read. Might you have time just to read my favorite essay? I would really love to hear your perspective." He will probably agree to that, so get that lunch meeting on the schedule and remember to mention, by the way, that you are buying!

When you meet together, it is imperative that you do more asking and listening than talking. Reconsidering one's view on the text of Scripture is a major undertaking, but especially for a Minister of the Word. Also, be sure to avoid overly-charged rhetoric. If you bring words like "liberal" or "heresy" to the table, your Pastor's defenses will immediately go up, and the level of trust you once enjoyed with him might decrease. Remember, this is your first conversation about the topic and, if you stay calm and respectful, there will most likely be more to come.

In taking up this discussion with your Pastor, you will need to remember and be content with the fact that it is your Pastor and Elders' responsibility to determine which version is used in the pulpit ministry of your church. If there is no openness to change, you should not push the matter. Rather, you should begin considering your ability to remain in your church as a faithful member while holding a different opinion on this particular issue. If you cannot do this (due to conscience), politely request that your membership be transferred to a nearby church of like faith and practice. The online "TR-friendly Church Directory" may be a helpful resource in such a case.

Advice to the Average Pastor

The editors of this book have slightly different experiences when it comes to shepherding their flocks over the years, but each has succeeded in helping those under their ministerial charge to understand and, for the most part, accept that only the Received Text of the Old and New Testaments will be used in the pulpit ministry of their particular churches. Your situation is, obviously, *your situation*, and we can only therefore offer generic advice when it comes to explaining the TR position to your church or, perhaps, leading your church to change its position.

Step one: Evaluate your congregation. How much do they actually know about the doctrine of Bibliology? How many translations are represented in the pews on any given Sunday? Do your members use those translations for specific reasons, or did they simply "inherit" them from their parents or the previous Pastor? Likewise, give careful consideration to the understanding and ability of your fellow church officers. Whatever changes you wish to implement in the church should be made *together*, so invest some time prayerfully evaluating your situation before you say a single word.

Step two: Offer a personal testimony. Before your next leadership meeting, ask for ten minutes on the agenda to offer a personal testimony about your views on the text. Offering a brief testimony is, of course, a far more personal (i.e., less threatening) event than scheduling an unexpected Sunday School series on New Testament textual criticism. It also establishes a certain rapport, or level of personal trust, before complicated (or potentially contentious) discussions arise.

Carefully prepare your testimony ahead of time, leaving out overly technical details, and ask a ministerial peer to review it for appropriateness of tone. The main purpose of the testimony is to explain how your acceptance of the TR has strengthened your faith and solidified your confidence as a teacher of God's Word. After you share your testimony with the Elders, plenty of time should be allowed for them to ask questions, and you should encourage them to go home and study the matter themselves for a season.

Step three: Equip your elders. If your Elders want to study the matter independently (not all of them will), they will most likely go home and start typing phrases into an internet search engine. It would therefore be wise to prepare in advance a list of resources for them so they do not get lost in the weeds. Do not overwhelm them. Two or three "pro" and "con" resources should be more than enough. A list of helpful books, websites, etc. will be appended after this essay to assist you in choosing some resources.

Different elders will not only have differing levels of interest in the topic, but also varied intellectual ability when it comes to understanding the issues involved; so do not expect them all to master the material. It is enough that they endeavor to understand the basic points of debate and the final options from which to choose: Received Text, Majority Text, or the Modern Critical Text.

Undoubtedly, not all will agree with your position, and it is not important that they do. The issue at hand is only this: Will the Elders support the Pastor in his use of a TR translation? If not, you have more work to do explaining the issues and your convictions. If so, the question quickly becomes, "How shall we explain this coming change to the congregation?"

Step four: Shepherd the flock. Your congregation will probably be less theologically capable than your Elders, so you should be wise in your approach. Sometimes a simple statement will suffice, such as, "After much personal study, the Pastor has come to believe that a translation based on the traditional text is more accurate than the one he previously used in the pulpit. The Elders heartily support his position." If this approach is taken, the Pastor's "Personal testimony" might be made available for reading either in print or online.

A great way to begin this document would be, "As your Pastor, I wish to explain my views on the text of the Bible. I am not asking that you agree with me and will never insist that you switch your preferred Bible version to remain a member of this church, but I do hope you will take the time to understand my personal convictions."

If there seems to be some great interest after the announcement, a class on Bibliology may be appropriate. Try to keep it short (four to six weeks), lest any be given the wrong impression that the Bible version debate has become your "personal pet peeve" or, worse, is about to become the center of your church's identity and ministry. This mistake will only play into the hands of divisive critics who will see this change as problematic. The most important step is simply this:

Step five: Make the change. Yes, things may "sound" different for a few weeks (visitors will *not* notice that, by the way), but the members will eventually become accustomed to the new version being used. There is, therefore, no need to draw undue attention to the change by regularly comparing the new version to the one previously used. Just make the change and move along in your ministry.

In fact, with your increased confidence in the text that you now preach, your people will undoubtedly come to love the change that has been made (albeit for only experiential reasons, as they profit from your increased unction in the pulpit).

Step six: Handle criticism well. As either explicitly mentioned or alluded to in several of the essays in this volume, holding to the

TR position will sometimes attract harsh criticisms. Some of these criticisms might be well-informed, while others might be hollow, emotional, and even irrational. How you react to such criticisms not only speaks volumes as to your level of Christian maturity, but also to the intellectual integrity of your convictions on the text.

We who accept and use the traditional text have scripture, theology, reason, and history on our side. Always remember that, and refuse to be drawn into childish squabblings. Your calm confidence will be noticed and, if God so wills, may even cause your opponents to re-examine their own position on the issue. If not, that is ultimately their problem and not yours.

Conclusion

These steps, of course, are only suggestive and by no means exhaustive. Every situation is different. Nevertheless, we offer them to you as those who have proven their usefulness on the apologetic battlefield.

Should you have any questions, the editors of this anthology would happily make themselves available for private correspondence. Send them an email at anthology.tr@gmail.com and they will do their best to assist you. Keep the faith, dear reader, and rest assured: God has kept his Word pure in all ages.

A Select Annotated Bibliography

Booklets, Pamphlets, Tracts

Anderson, G. W. and D. E. Anderson. *A Textual Key to the New Testament: A List of Omissions and Changes*. London: Trinitarian Bible Society, 1993.

This tract provides a helpful list highlighting six hundred and fifty places in the New Testament where the modern critical text differs from the traditional text.

McShaffrey, Christian M. *How the Holy Bible Came to Be: An Elementary Introduction to the Doctrine of Believing Bibliology*. London: Trinitarian Bible Society, 2021.

This booklet provides a simple, accessible, and popular presentation, appropriate for all ages, of how the traditional text of the Bible came to be and why it is important for believers to uphold it today.

Watts, Malcolm. *The Lord Gave the Word: A Study in the History of the Biblical Text*. London: Trinitarian Bible Society, 1998.

This booklet presents an overview of the transmission of the text of Scripture which defends the traditional text and concludes with preferential arguments for the KJV.

Protestant Orthodox Defenses of the Traditional Text

Owen, John. "Of the Divine Original, Authority, Self-Evidencing Light, and Power of the Scriptures." Pages 281–344 in vol. 16 of *The Works of John Owen*. Edinburgh/Carlisle: Banner of Truth reprint, 1968.

John Owen presents a Protestant orthodox Bibliology stressing the authority, inspiration, infallibility, and self-evidencing nature of Scripture as preserved in the faithful apographs (copies).

_____. "Integrity and Purity of the Hebrew and Greek Text." Pages 345–421 in vol. 16 of *The Works of John Owen*. Edinburgh/Carlisle: Banner of Truth reprint, 1968.

John Owen wrote this work in response to the publication of Brian Walton's "Polyglot," an early attempt at a critical text of Scripture. Owen defends the traditional text as preserved in extant copies.

Turretin, Francis. *Institutes of Elenctic Theology*. Pages 55-167 in vol. 1. Translated by George M. Giger. Edited by James T. Dennison, Jr. Phillipsburg, NJ: Presbyterian and Reformed Publishing Company, 1992.

Turretin, one of the great leaders of Calvinist orthodoxy and scholasticism, presents a classic Protestant view of Bibliology.

Whitaker, William. *A Disputation on Holy Scripture Against the Papists especially Bellarmine and Stapleton*. Translated and Edited by William Fitzgerald. Orlando, FL: Soli Deo Gloria Publications, 2005.

Whitaker presents a standard defense of the Protestant canon and original language text of the Bible, over against the Roman Catholic view.

Nineteenth-Century Defenses of the Traditional Text

Burgon, John W. *The Revision Revised*. Collingswood, NJ: Dean Burgon Society Press, 2000.

This is a reprint of Dean Burgon's vigorous defense of the traditional text of Scripture, underlying the KJV, against the English Revised Version of 1881 and the modern text of Westcott and Hort. It consists of three articles which originally appeared in *The Quarterly Review*: (1) The Greek New Testament; (2) The New English Version; (3) Westcott and Hort's New Textual

Theory.

Dabney, Robert L. "The Doctrinal Various Readings of the New Testament Greek," Pages 350–390 in vol. 1 of *Discussions*. Harrisonburg, VA: Sprinkle Reprint, 1982.

The stalwart Presbyterian pastor and theologian defends the traditional text of Scripture, including the *Comma Johanneum* (1 John 5:7–8), against the modern critical text.

_____. "The Revised Version of the New Testament," Pages 391–398 in vol. 1 of *Discussions*. Harrisonburg, VA: Sprinkle Reprint, 1982.

Dabney reviews and finds fault with the English Revised Version (1881).

Twentieth Century Defenses of the Traditional Text

Hills, Edward F. *The King James Version Defended*, 4th ed. Des Moines, IA: The Christian Research Press, 1956, 1984.

Hills, a credentialed text critic, presents a groundbreaking defense of the *Textus Receptus* underlying the New Testament translation of the King James Version and articulates a Reformed doctrine of the divine preservation of Scripture based on "the logic of faith."

_____. *Believing Bible Study*. Junction City, OR: Eye Opener Publishers, 1967.

This book provides a popular presentation of Hills' views of the text, including his contention that the believer cannot approach Scripture without presuppositions guided by faith.

_____. *"Introduction,"* Pages 17–72 in *The Last Twelve Verses of Mark*. Lafayette, IN: Sovereign Grace Publishers, 2000.

This essay, composed of three chapters, offers an approving introduction to Burgon's work on Mark's ending. It begins, "Every faithful Christian must reckon seriously with the teaching of Christ concerning the providential preservation of Scripture" (17).

Letis, Theodore P., ed. *The Majority Text: Essays and Reviews in the Continuing Debate*. Institute for Biblical Textual Studies, 1987.

Various essays and book reviews, compiled and edited by Letis, which critique the modern critical text and defend the Received Text.

_____. *Edward Freer Hills's Contribution to the Revival of the Ecclesiastical Text*. Philadelphia, PA: The Institute for Renaissance and Reformation Biblical Studies, 1987.

Letis offers an appreciative survey of how E. F. Hills challenged

Protestant compromise in abandoning the traditional text.

———. *The Ecclesiastical Text: Text Criticism, Biblical Authority, and the Popular Mind*. The Institute for Renaissance and Reformation Biblical Studies, 1997.

This book is a collection of essays and book reviews by Letis from various academic journals on the topic of textual criticism. Letis defends the traditional text, which he refers to as the "ecclesiastical text," over against the modern critical text. Noteworthy is his discussion of the role of B. B. Warfield and the search for the *autograph* in the evangelical abandonment of the Protestant emphasis on the preserved *apographa*.

Resources for Understanding Twenty-First Century Modern Textual Criticism

Riddle, Jeffrey T. "The Coherence-Based Genealogical Method (CBGM): The Newest 'New' Method." *Quarterly Record*, No. 635 (2021): 12–19.

This article offers a succinct summary and evaluation of the new CBGM method, which is being applied to the modern critical text of the Greek NT.

Shah, Abidan Paul. *Changing the Goalpost of New Testament Textual Criticism*. Eugene, OR: Wipf & Stock, 2020.

This is an edition of Shah's doctoral dissertation under Byzantine Priority advocate Maurice Robinson. Shah examines the "radical shift" in the goal of contemporary textual criticism, as it has abandoned any confidence in reconstructing the original autograph and now seeks only an unstable approximation of the "initial text." He also provides a critique of the Coherence-Based Genealogical Method and warns of the doctrinal and practical consequences of this shift in text critical goals and methodology.

Historical Theological Resources on Text and Bibliology

Brash, Richard F. *The Reformed Doctrine of the Providential Preservation of Scripture*, 1588-1687. Philadelphia, PA: Westminster Theological Seminary, 2017.

_____. "Ad Fontes!—The Concept of the 'Originals' of Scripture in Seventeenth Century Reformed Orthodoxy," *WTJ*, No. 81 (2019): 123–139.

In his Master's thesis and in this academic article, Brash demonstrates that the Protestant orthodox did not think it was their task to reconstruct the autographs, but to affirm a "practical univocity" between the autographs and the printed editions of the faithful apographs.

Milne, Garnet Howard. *Has the Bible been kept pure? The Westminster Confession of Faith and the providential preservation of Scripture.* Garnet Howard Milne, 2017.

A Reformed minister from New Zealand surveys classic Reformed religious epistemology, as expressed in the *Westminster Confession of Faith* (1.8), which recognizes the pure and preserved text of Scripture as the *principium cognoscendi externum*.

Muller, Richard A. *Post-Reformation Reformed Dogmatics*, Vol. 2. Holy Scripture: The Cognitive Foundation of Theology series. Grand Rapids, MI: Baker Books, 1993.

Muller offers a compelling in-depth survey of the Reformation and Post-Reformation Protestant orthodox approach to Scripture, noting their emphasis not on the reconstruction of the autographs but the preservation of the text in the apographs.

Riddle, Jeffrey T. "Erasmus Anecdotes," *Puritan Reformed Journal*, Vol. 9, No. 1 (2017): 101–112.

This article shows how modern scholars have promoted various legendary anecdotes about Erasmus (like the "rash wager" anecdote regarding the addition of the *Comma Johanneum* to his printed edition of the Greek NT) in order to undermine the reliability of the *Textus Receptus*.

_____. "Calvin and Text Criticism," *Puritan Reformed Journal*, Vol. 9, No. 2 (2017): 128–146.

This article demonstrates that the mature Calvin was well

aware of various controversies regarding textual variants in the NT, and yet he warmly embraced readings found in the *Textus Receptus*.

Majority Text and Byzantine Priority Defenses of the Traditional Text

Pickering, Wilbur N. *Identity of the New Testament Text II*. 3rd Edition. Wipf and Stock Publishers, 2003.

A missionary to Brazil and expert in linguistics, Pickering defends the "Majority Text" against the modern critical text.

Robinson, Maurice A. "The Case for Byzantine Priority," Pages 533–586 in *The New Testament in the Original Greek: Byzantine Textform 2005*. Arranged and compiled by Maurice A. Robinson and William G. Pierpont. Southborough, MA: Chilton Book Publishing, 2005.

Robinson, a long-time defender of the "Byzantine Text," presents a sustained argument for the priority of this text and a critique of the canons of modern textual criticism.

Sturz, Harry A. *The Byzantine Text-Type & New Testament Textual Criticism*. Nashville, TN: Thomas Nelson, 1984.

Sturz demonstrates that Byzantine readings which support the traditional text are found in the earliest extant papyri manuscripts, thus completely undermining the theories of Westcott and Hort which suggested that the Byzantine text is late and secondary.

Van Bruggen, Jakob. *The Ancient Text of the New Testament.* Premier, 1976.

A respected Dutch scholar offers a convincing defense of the traditional text of the Greek NT.

Resources on the Ending of Mark

Black, D. A., ed., *Perspectives on the Ending of Mark*, Nashville, TN: B & H Academic, 2008.

This collection of essays came from a conference held at Southeastern Baptist Theological Seminary (Wake Forest, NC). It includes chapters from Dan Wallace ("reasoned eclecticism"), Maurice Robinson (Byzantine text), Keith Elliot ("thoroughgoing eclecticism"), and D. A. Black (multiple authorship theory). Wallace and Elliot reject Mark 16:9–20 as authentic, while Robinson and Black defend it.

Burgon, John W. *The Last Twelve Verses of Mark.* Lafayette, IN: Sovereign Grace Publishers, 2000.

This is a reprint of Dean Burgon's classic defense of the traditional text of Mark's Ending (Mark 16:9–20).

Farmer, William R. *The Last Twelve Verses of Mark*. Cambridge: Cambridge University Press, 1974.

A respected mainstream academic scholar and proponent of Matthean Priority defends the authenticity of the traditional ending of Mark.

Lunn, Nicholas P. *The Original Ending of Mark: A New Case for the Authenticity of Mark 16:9–20*. Eugene, OR: Pickwick Publications, 2014.

Lunn, a Translation Consultant with Wycliffe Bible Translators, UK, and Tutor at Spurgeon's College (London), provides an extensive argument, based on both external and internal evidence, in favor of the authenticity of Mark's traditional ending.

Riddle, Jeffrey T. "The Ending of Mark as a Canonical Crisis," *Puritan Reformed Journal*, Vol. 10, No. 1 (2018): 31–54.

This article calls for a renewed consensus that the traditional ending is the authentic and fitting canonical conclusion to Mark's Gospel.

Resources on the *Pericope Adulterae* (John 7:53—8:11)

Black, David Alan and Jacob N. Cerone. *The Pericope of the Adulteress in Contemporary Research*. London: Bloomsbury, 2016.

This collection of essays came from a conference held at South-eastern Baptist Theological Seminary (Wake Forest, NC). Two contributors (John David Punch and Maurice Robinson) defend inclusion of the pericope, while three contributors (Tommy Wasserman, Jennifer Knust, and Chris Keith) make the case against its authenticity.

Knust, Jennifer and Tommy Wasserman. *To Cast the First Stone: The Transmission of A Gospel Story*. Princeton, NJ: Princeton University Press, 2019.

Two mainstream modern textual scholars who do not affirm the authenticity of John 7:53-8:11 nevertheless provide a helpful survey of the passage's reception history in the Christian tradition.

Punch, John David. *The Pericope Adulterae: Theories of Insertion and Omission: An Academic Essay in Theology*. Lambert Academic Publishing, 2012.

This is a printed version of Punch's 2010 dissertation, completed at the Radbound University (Nijmegen, Netherlands). Punch presents arguments for and against the pericope's authenticity. In the end, he suggests that internal evidence argues in favor of its authenticity and suggests the passage was most likely omitted due to "ecclesiastical suppression." Note: A digital version is available for free download from the Radbound Repository.

Resources on Other Disputed Texts

Carson, Cottrel. "Acts 8:37—A Textual Reexamination." *Union Seminary Quarterly Review*, 51:1–2 (1997): 57–78.

A mainstream academic scholar reexamines Acts 8:37 and argues for its authenticity.

Mahlen, Brett and Christian McShaffrey. "Doxology or Devil? A Case for the Longer Ending of the Lord's Prayer." *Puritan Reformed Journal*, Vol. 13, No. 2 (2021): 21–31.

Two ministers in the Orthodox Presbyterian Church present an argument in favor of the authenticity of the doxology of the Lord's Prayer (Matthew 6:13b) and its continued inclusion in the catechisms of the church.

McDonald, Grantley. *Biblical Criticism in Early Modern Europe: Erasmus, the Johannine Comma, and the Trinitarian Debate*. Cambridge: Cambridge University Press, 2016.

Though the author does not embrace the authenticity of the *Comma Johanneum* (1 John 5:7b–8a), he provides a helpful survey of the reception history of this passage in the Christian tradition, noting its long standing as a flashpoint in Trinitarian controversy.

Text and Translation Issues

Einwechter, William O. *English Bible Translations: By What Standard?* Pensacola, FL: Chapel Library, 2010.

A booklet written on a popular level defending the principle of a literal translation philosophy (over against dynamic equivalence) and the traditional text (over against the modern critical text). It concludes by expressing preference for the KJV while also denouncing KJV-Onlyism.

Mcgregor, Alan J. *Three Modern Versions: A Critical Assessment of the NIV, ESV, and NKJV*. The Bible League, 2004.

Macgregor offers a charitable but challenging assessment of three modern versions and defends his preference for the KJV.

Van Bruggen, Jakob. *The Future of the Bible*. Nashville, TN: Thomas Nelson, 1978.

This book critiques the proliferation of contemporary Bible translations in the evangelical marketplace.

Critiques of the Modern Historical Critical Method

Linnemann, Eta. *Historical Criticism of the Bible: Methodology of Ideology? Reflections of a Bultmannian Turned Evangelical*. Translated by Robert Yarbrough. Grand Rapids, MI: Kregel Academic,

2001.

Linnemann tells her story first of being trained as a scholar steeped in the modern historical-critical method and then her conversion to Christ, which resulted in her rejection of this method as incompatible with her Christian faith.

Maier, Gerhard. *The End of the Historical-Critical Method.* St. Louis, MO: Concordia Publishing House, 1977.

A German scholar declares the modern historical-critical method to be a "dead-end" and incompatible with those who uphold the infallibility of Scripture.

Yarbrough, Robert Y. *Clash of Visions: Populism and Elitism in New Testament Theology.* Geanies House, Fern, Ross-shire, Great Britain: Christian Focus, 2019.

This short work is taken from the Gheens Lectures given at Southern Baptist Theological Seminary (Louisville, KY) by Yarbrough, a noted PCA scholar. He identifies a "clash" between the modern academic approach to the Bible and the way ordinary believers and Christian scholars approach the Bible.

Websites that Defend the Traditional Text

Trinitarian Bible Society	tbsbibles.org
Text & Translation	textandtranslation.org
Stylos	jeffriddle.net
Textus Receptus Bibles	textusreceptusbibles.com
Confessional Bibliology	confessionalbibliology.com
Textus Receptus Wiki	textus-receptus.com/wiki
The Young, Textless, and Reformed	youngtextlessreformed.com

About The Greater Heritage

Mission
The Greater Heritage is a Christian publishing ministry that equips believers for an abundant life of service, personal spiritual growth and character development.

What We Do
The Greater Heritage publishes original articles, books, Bible studies and church resources. All of its books are made entirely in the USA.

Want to publish with us? Inquire at:
The Greater Heritage
1170 Tree Swallow Dr., Suite 309
Winter Springs, Florida 32708
info@thegreaterheritage.com
www.thegreaterheritage.com

Find more books and our latest catalog online at:
www.thegreaterheritage.com/shop